Dear Pam

ON THE TRACK

SENIOR AUTHORS
Virginia A. Arnold
Carl B. Smith

LITERATURE CONSULTANTS
Joan I. Glazer
Margaret H. Lippert

READING
EXPRESS
MACMILLAN

Macmillan Publishing Company
New York

Collier Macmillan Publishers
London

Macmillan Publishing Company
866 Third Avenue
New York, N.Y. 10022
Collier Macmillan Canada, Inc.

Printed in the United States of America

ISBN 0-02-160080-5

9 8 7 6 5

ACKNOWLEDGMENTS

The publisher gratefully acknowledges permission to reprint the following copyrighted material:

"Adventure in the Night" is adapted from THE MOUSE AND THE MOTORCYCLE by Beverly Cleary. Copyright © 1965 by Beverly Cleary. By permission of William Morrow & Company and Hamish Hamilton Ltd.

"Bambi's Children" by Felix Salten has been adapted by Margaret H. Lippert. Used by permission of Dr. Veit Wyler.

"Burton and Dudley" is adapted from BURTON AND DUDLEY by Marjorie Weinman Sharmat. Copyright © 1975 by Marjorie Weinman Sharmat. Used by permission of Holiday House, Inc.

"Changing" from YELLOW BUTTER PURPLE JELLY RED JAM BLACK BREAD by Mary Ann Hoberman. Copyright © 1981 by Mary Ann Hoberman. Reprinted by permission of Viking Penguin Inc.

"The Frog and I" from IN ONE DOOR AND OUT THE OTHER: A Book of Poems by Aileen Fisher (Thomas Y. Crowell Co.). Text Copyright © 1969 by Aileen Fisher. By permission of Harper & Row, Publishers, Inc.

"The Hare" is excerpted from "The Hare" by a 9th Grade Student in Swaziland and appears in ROSE, WHERE DID YOU GET THAT RED? by Kenneth Koch. Copyright © 1973 by Kenneth Koch. Reprinted by permission of Random House, Inc. and Kenneth Koch.

"This Tooth" from ME! by Lee Bennett Hopkins. Copyright © 1970, 1974 by Lee Bennett Hopkins. Reprinted by permission of Curtis Brown, Ltd.

Cover Design: Bass and Goldman Associates

Illustration Credits: Michael W. Adams, 86–88, 90–92; Alex Bloch, 106–110, 113–115, 117–119; Gwen Connelly, 74–76, 78, 81, 83, 84–85; Rick L. Cooley, 40–42, 44–45, 47–49; Len Ebert, 152–156, 158–162; Betsy Feeney, 94–96, 98–99, 101–102; Terrence Fehr, 32–36; Paulette Giguere, 104–105; Gay Holland, 223–228; Peter Kruse, 10–20; Diana Magnuson, 194–195; Charles McVicker, 174, 176–182; Meryle Meisler, 230–231; Ted Minon, 175; Carl Molno, 30–31, 50–57, 72–73, 142–146, 148–150, 211, 221, 232–243, 245–256; Sal Murdocca, 58–71; Jody Silver, 22–29; Samantha Carol Smith, 185–188, 190, 192, 193; Lynn Sweat, 134–136, 166–173, 184, 196–205, 207–209; Gary Undercuffler, 122–128, 130–133.

Cover Photo: © Janeart Ltd.

Photo Credits: © All–American Soap Box Derby, 137R, 138, 141. © George Ancona, 34–36. © Joseph A. Dichello, Jr., 139. Duomo Photography, Inc.: Dan Helms, 120. The Image Bank: © Mel DiGiacomo, 214R; © Nieke Haas, 213; © R. Sauter, 140. © James M. Mejuto, 137L. © Mary Messenger, 171. Monkmeyer Press Photo Service: © Hugh Rogers, 216, 218R. New York Special Olympics, © 212B, 212T, 214L, 215. Photo Researchers, Inc.: © Lowell J. Georgia, 172; © Richard Hutchings, 8. H. Armstrong Roberts: © S. Feld, 217; © M. Roessler, 168. Stock Boston: © Doug Greene, 1969; © Suzanne Szasz, 52–56. Taurus Photos: © Reggie Tucker, 170.

Contents

LEVEL 8, UNIT 1: All About Me **8**

PREPARING FOR READING (Short Vowel: /e/e) **10**
Burton and Dudley, *a story by Marjorie Sharmat* **12**

PREPARING FOR READING (Short Vowel: /a/a) **22**
No Fair Friday, *a story by Cynthia Rothman* **24**

PREPARING FOR READING (Number of Syllables) **30**
On the Team, *a photo-story by Stephanie Calmenson* **32**

* **Writing Activity:** *Write a Factual Paragraph*........ **38**

PREPARING FOR READING (Short Vowel: /u/u) **40**
Larry's Big Race, *a story by Johanna Hurwitz* **42**

PREPARING FOR READING (Short Vowel: /i/i) **50**
Keeping Your Best Smile, *a photo-essay by Adair Sirota*..... **52**

PREPARING FOR READING (Short Vowel: /o/o)   58

A Huge Toothache, *a mystery play by Susan Nanus*   60

This Tooth, *a poem by Lee Bennett Hopkins*   72

PREPARING FOR READING (Number of Syllables)   74

Friends Through a Storm, *a story by Argentina Palacios* . .   76

PREPARING FOR READING (Number of Syllables)   86

A Special Kind of Winner, *a biographical sketch*
by Cynthia Rothman   88

PREPARING FOR READING (Short Vowel: /i/i)   94

Two Is Better Than One, *a story by Antoinette Bement* . . .   96

Changing, *a poem by Mary Ann Hoberman*   104

PREPARING FOR READING (Short Vowel: /u/u)   106

Hans Clodhopper, *a Hans Christian Andersen fairy tale*
adapted by Margaret H. Lippert   108

LEVEL 8, UNIT 2: Racing On. **120**

PREPARING FOR READING (Short Vowel: /ə/a,e,o,u) **122**

The Eddie-Teddie Racer, *a story by Johanna Hurwitz*. **124**

PREPARING FOR READING (Short Vowel: /ə/e,i,o) **134**

Soap Box Derby, *a photo-essay by Anne Rockwell* **136**

PREPARING FOR READING (Prefix: un-) **142**

A Day at the Race, *a story by Stephanie Calmenson*. **144**

PREPARING FOR READING (Possessive Nouns) **152**

Grandpa's Special Ride, *an autobiographical story*
by Earl G. Robbins **154**

✳ **Writing Activity:** *Write a Description*. **164**

PREPARING FOR READING (Possessive Nouns) **166**

At the Rodeo, *a photo-essay by Debra Desideri*. **168**

PREPARING FOR READING (Short Vowel: /ə/a,e,o). **174**

The Pony Express, *a historical article by Lisbeth Stern*. **176**

PREPARING FOR READING (Possessive Nouns) **184**

Jumping Jennifer, *a story by Nancy Whisler* **186**

The Frog and I, *a poem by Aileen Fisher* **194**

PREPARING FOR READING (Prefix: *re-*) **196**

Bambi's Children, *a story by Felix Salten*
adapted by Margaret H. Lippert **198**

PREPARING FOR READING (Prefix: *re-*) **210**

Special Sports for Special People, *a photo-essay*
by Ada B. Litchfield **212**

PREPARING FOR READING (Prefixes: *re-, un-*) **220**

The Tortoise and the Hare, *an Aesop fable*
retold by Karen Young **222**

The Hare, *a poem by a ninth-grade student in Swaziland* **230**

STRETCHER: **Adventure in the Night,**
a story from The Mouse and the Motorcycle, *by Beverly Cleary* **232**

Glossary **244**

UNIT ONE   LEVEL 8

ALL
ABOUT
ME

PREPARING FOR READING

Learning Vocabulary

Listen for the short vowel.

hen

| bed | blew | presents | there |
| dear | eat | left | tent |

Read the sentences.

1. <u>Fresh</u> air and exercise help people <u>relax</u>.
2. People should not be <u>pushed</u> into too much exercise at one time.
3. If you run around and scream <u>loudly</u>, you will be very <u>tired</u>.
4. <u>Always</u> relax before you get too tired.

| fresh | relax | pushed | loudly |
| tired | always |

Developing Background

Read and talk.

Walking

Walking is good exercise. If you are always rushing around in your work, a walk in the fresh air can help you relax. You can walk in all kinds of weather. You can walk a little, or you can walk a long time. Don't walk too long at first, or you will get too tired. Look around as you walk. See your world and relax.

In *Burton and Dudley*, Dudley gets Burton to take a walk. Will Burton like it?

Dudley Possum walked over to his friend Burton's house. "Burton, are you home?" called Dudley.

"I am always home," said Burton, and he let Dudley in.

"I came to see if you might want to take a walk with me," said Dudley.

"A walk?" asked Burton.

"Yes," said Dudley. "A walk. You know, when you move one foot and then the next."

"Yes, yes, I know what a walk is," said Burton. "I don't take walks."

"But," said Dudley, "I want you to try. You don't get out each day. You should always get fresh air and exercise."

"I like to see the animals take their walks. They can have all the fresh air and exercise. I don't need it," said Burton.

"Please take a walk with me," said Dudley, with a smile.

"I will, if you sit with me for now and put your feet up," said Burton. "Look out at the trees and be happy to be here in the quiet house."

"I will do it," said Dudley.

Burton and Dudley had their feet up and looked out at the trees.

"This is what I like. This is for me," said Burton. "Now relax, Dudley. You must relax."

"Yes," said Dudley.

After a time, Dudley said, "Now our time to relax is over. Will you take that walk with me now?"

"I will," Burton said.

Then he and Dudley began to walk.

"I know of a special tree on a farm in the country," said Dudley. "We will walk to it."

Burton and Dudley walked on.

"The birds are singing loudly. They make me so happy," said Dudley.

Burton and Dudley walked on, and then Burton said, "I am very tired. Please may we stop for a time?"

"Yes," said Dudley. "You don't always get so much fresh air and exercise. You are not ready for so much fresh air."

Burton began to relax.

"The clouds look pretty up there," said Burton. "I have not seen the sky look so pretty."

Then Burton got up.

"I am ready to go on now," he said.

Burton and Dudley went on to the farm. Then Burton looked at Dudley.

"Do you know where I might get a drink?" he asked.

"There is fresh water on the farm. I will show you where," said Dudley.

Dudley found the place for Burton and helped him get a drink.

They walked on and on. Soon Burton had to stop.

"I am tired," he said. "Please, can you help me?"

"I can't," said Dudley, "because I am tired now, too."

"You are tired?" asked Burton. "You with all the walks in the fresh air and all the exercise. You are tired?"

"Yes," said Dudley. "I am TIRED! That is all the exercise for me. I can't go on."

Burton said, "Now it is my turn to help you exercise, so please get up."

Dudley did.

"Now I will help you to move your feet. Are you ready?" asked Burton.

"I am ready," said Dudley.

Burton pushed Dudley, and Dudley moved his feet.

"It works!" Burton screamed, loudly.

Burton pushed Dudley up and down and through the woods.

"Do you want to stop now?" asked Dudley.

"I am not tired," said Burton. "I like this walk. I remember birds singing loudly, pretty clouds in the sky, and a drink of fresh water on a country farm. I have not seen these things before. I want to see all there is to see. I want to see the world."

"You may want to see the world, but I want to go home, Burton," said Dudley.

So through the woods, up and down, Burton pushed Dudley to his house.

"You must be happy to be home," said Dudley.

"No, I am not," said Burton. "Please come for a walk now. I must go to new places to see different things."

"We can go next summer," said Dudley, with a smile.

"Yes, but I hope next summer comes soon," said Burton.

Then Dudley asked, "For now, may I have something to put my feet up on so I can sit here and look at the trees?"

"Make my home your home," said Burton.

Dudley looked out.

"This is what I like. This is for me," he said, with a smile.

Questions

Read and think.
1. What did Dudley want to do?
2. Who got tired first?
   Then who got tired?
3. What did Dudley want to do when they got to Burton's house?
4. Why didn't Burton get tired as they walked home?

PREPARING FOR READING

Learning Vocabulary

Listen for short vowels.

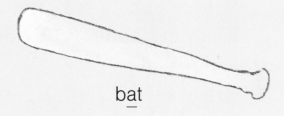

bat

plane	after	say	swam
rabbit	saw	pass	scary

Read the sentences.

1. My class at school had a special fair.
2. I was sick, but I wanted to come.
3. The fair showed people how to relax and feel well through exercise.

class   fair   sick   feel   well

Developing Background

Read and talk.

A Fair

Our school has a fair each winter. Last winter we had a book fair. At the music fair, each boy or girl made an instrument and we played music together. The travel fair was special because we showed different places around the world we wanted to go. This time, the school nurse will help us and we will have a health fair. What do you do at a health fair? Read *No Fair Friday* and find out.

23

NO FAIR FRIDAY

CYNTHIA ROTHMAN

All the children looked up.

"Who put that up?" asked Inez.

"Why can't we have our school health fair on Friday?" asked Jordan.

Then Miyo came running up to them.

"Mrs. Storm didn't feel well. She went home sick."

So that was it. Mrs. Storm was the school nurse. She was the one who was going to run the school health fair. If Mrs. Storm couldn't be in school, there couldn't be a fair.

"*No fair Friday* is right. It isn't fair that we can't have a fair on Friday," said Peter.

"The nurse is there when we don't feel well and need her to take care of us. We can help her now that she is sick," said Amanda.

"But how?" asked Rosa.

"We can take her place and put together the school health fair. We can work as a team," said Amanda.

"Now we have to find out what Mr. Small says about this," said Peter.

They asked Mr. Small, their teacher.

"There are many things you are going to have to do to be ready for a fair on Friday," he said. "You will have to get all the needed books, movies, and pictures. Each station at the fair will have to have a boy or girl by it. He or she will show things to each class as it walks by."

The team was very quiet.

"Well," Mr. Small went on, "do you want to help with the fair?" All the children said they wanted to try.

The children worked before school. They worked after school. They worked at home before bedtime. They got together all kinds of books, pictures, and movies.

By Friday, every station was ready. Each class came to see and learn at the fair. They walked to every station.

Inez had a collection of pictures at her station. They showed things to do each day for good health.

Miyo's station showed how exercise can make you feel good. She had many exercise books for the children to read. There was one about running and one about swimming. Peter did some of his special gymnastics for each class to see.

Amanda showed movies about the different kinds of food needed to help children grow. One of the movies was called *Eat Right, Be Well.*

Rosa had a ruler to measure each of the children. The children liked to see how big they were now.

Some children put on a funny play called *See It Now!* about good eye care and the need for glasses.

What a day! There were so many things to learn.

At last the fair was over. Some of the children were sad that it was over so soon.

Then Mr. Small came up. "Look who came to the health fair," he said. It was Mrs. Storm, the school nurse. Now she wanted to speak to them.

She said, "I am so happy that you wanted to help me when I was sick. I thank you for the work you did to help make this a very special school health fair."

"Can we have a fair next Friday, Mrs. Storm?" asked Jordan.

Mrs. Storm had a big smile. "Well, no fair on Friday, but very soon."

Questions

Read and think.
1. Why did Mrs. Storm go home?
2. What did the children do to help Mrs. Storm?
3. What were some of the things the children showed at the fair?
4. Why did the children want to help Mrs. Storm?

PREPARING FOR READING

Learning Vocabulary

Listen for syllables.

hamster

ham'·ster

yellow	wish	station	kick
funny	ostrich	game	turtle

Read the sentences.

1. Your <u>body</u> needs exercise for good health.
2. It is <u>better</u> to exercise a little than to do too much.
3. If you <u>ache</u> as you exercise, it is <u>best</u> to stop.
4. <u>Think</u> about the kinds of exercise you can do for good health.

body   better   ache   best   think

Developing Background

Read and talk.

The Doctor

Many people go to the doctor when they don't feel well, but you should go when you feel good, too. If you are going to do much running, biking, or some kinds of fast exercise, you should have the doctor take a look at you. First, he will find out how well your heart and lungs work. Then, he will see how your muscles feel when you exercise. Last, he will help you pick the best kinds of exercise for you. In *On the Team*, Anita needs to exercise. What does she do?

ON THE TEAM

Stephanie Calmenson

Exercise! Exercise! We all like to exercise!

One exercise class likes singing when it runs in place. Some people like to play music on the radio when they exercise. One of the important things to remember is that exercise can be something you like to do.

You do not need to go to a class to get your exercise. There are all kinds of things you can do. You can dance, race, walk, run, or go biking. John likes skiing best. His sister, Anita, likes to swim.

There was a time when Anita couldn't swim well. She wanted to be on the team, but she was not ready.

"Why don't you try to exercise?" asked her brother John. "Exercise will help you feel better."

Anita read a story about one of the swimming stars she liked best. The woman did exercises to feel better. These exercises helped her get ready for each swim race. So, Anita began to read different exercise books. Next she went to see Coach Browning at her school.

"Exercise will make your body strong, Anita. I think you can make the swim team if you try your best."

Coach Browning said that exercise helps muscles and lungs.

"Remember, Anita, your heart is one of your muscles, too. It is one of the very important muscles in your body. Your heart and lungs work together."

When she began to train, Coach Browning asked Anita, "Do you exercise each day?"

Anita said, "No."

"At first a little exercise each day is best. Try to walk as much as you can," said the coach. "That will be your first step. Then you can try to walk fast. Then you can try to run."

Anita was soon running for exercise. She went biking with John, too. Anita found many different kinds of exercises that she liked to do.

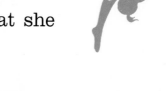

Now and then Anita got an ache. She had to stop and try to relax. Then the ache went away.

"An ache in your body will let you know that you have worked hard," said Coach Browning to Anita.

Anita got better and better each day.

"I think you are ready to try out for the swim team," said the coach.

"I know I am strong now," Anita said.

On the day of the tryout, Anita was a little scared. But she said to John, "I think I am going to make it."

When the tryout was over, Anita flew home. She had to let John know that she was on the team!

Every boy and girl should exercise. Remember that it is not hard to get your exercise every day. You may want to walk, not ride, when you can. You may want to join in and play if there is a game. Look for different kinds of exercises to do each day. You will feel better if you do!

Questions

Read and think.
1. What team did Anita want to join?
2. Who did Anita go to see for help?
3. What did Anita do to make her body strong?
4. How did Anita feel before the tryout?
   How did she feel after the tryout?

WRITING ACTIVITY

WRITE A FACTUAL PARAGRAPH

Prewrite

Burton, in "Burton and Dudley," didn't like to exercise very much. Anita, in "On the Team," had to learn how important exercise was if she wanted to be on the swim team. If you worked at a gym, you might have a little book about exercise for people who came to work out. The first paragraph in the book might tell about exercise, and why it is good for you.

You are going to write that paragraph on exercise. Before you write, think about who will read the paragraph. Some people like exercise, and some do not. You must have facts for both kinds of people. Try these things to help you find facts. Then write the facts in sentences for your paragraph.

1. Read the first three stories in this book.
2. Find a book about exercise to read.
3. Ask your friends what they think about exercise.

Write

1. Write your paragraph about exercise on your paper.
2. One of these sentences could be your first sentence.

   Exercise will make you feel better.
   Exercise is important for your good health!
3. Now write your facts about exercise from page 38.
4. Use your Glossary for help with spelling.
5. If you wish, you may draw some pictures of the exercises people might want to do.

Revise

Read your paragraph. Will people want to exercise after they read it? Did you write some facts from books and some facts from your friends? You may want to write some sentences now.

1. Did you indent the first word in your paragraph?
2. Did you start your sentences with capital letters and use the correct end punctuation?

PREPARING FOR READING

Learning Vocabulary

Listen for short vowels.

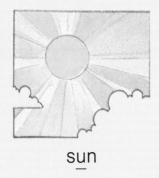

sun

thunder	run	blue	clouds
huge	busy	rush	bump

Read the sentences.

1. Do you <u>brush</u> every day and <u>chew</u> your food well?
2. If your <u>tooth</u> aches, you might feel as if you <u>hurt</u> all over.
3. Soon every tooth in your <u>mouth</u> may feel funny.

brush   chew   tooth   hurt   mouth

Developing Background

Read and talk.

The Dentist

Going to the dentist is important to your health. You should go before you get a cavity. If you wait too long to go, your tooth may have to come out. Every tooth in your mouth is important, because each one is needed to chew your food. Some people say, "Well, I brush every day." That is not all you must do. Your mouth is as important as your heart and lungs to your good health.

Larry Moss has a big race and a big cavity. What does he do in the story, *Larry's Big Race?*

LARRY'S BIG RACE

Johanna Hurwitz

Larry Moss liked ice skating and biking. Best of all Larry liked running.

"Running is very hard work," said Larry's friend Emily.

"It is hard work," said Larry, "but it is special for me. When I am running, I feel strong. My muscles help me to run like lightning."

"If you like to run so much, you should be in the school race," said Emily.

All the children at Larry's school were busy because of the race. The gymnastics teacher helped all the children work on their running.

"Not too fast," the teacher said. "You don't want to do too much before you are ready. You don't want to hurt the muscles in your legs. You must take care of your body before you race."

On the day of the school race, Larry was eating his eggs before he went to school. As he was eating, his mouth began to hurt. He couldn't chew well.

"Oh, oh, my tooth aches," he said.

"You might have a cavity," said his mother. "I will call and see if the dentist can take us right now."

"No, no," said Larry. "I can't go to the dentist today. Not today! I don't care if my tooth aches. If I don't chew, it will not hurt. I must run in the school race. I will go to the dentist after the race," he said to his mother.

But his mouth did hurt. It hurt very much. It was as if every tooth in his mouth had its own special ache. It hurt so much that Larry couldn't brush.

"If we go to the dentist right away, you can get to school in time," said Mrs. Moss. "You can't run well if your tooth aches."

Larry said, "Why now? This is not the right time for this."

"There is no right time for a tooth to ache," said Mrs. Moss. She called the dentist. "He can see us right now. Come on."

Mrs. Moss drove to the dentist. Dr. Winter did take Larry right away.

Larry said, "Can you help me, Dr. Winter? I have to get to school fast to be in a race."

"I will do the best I can. Now sit down and relax," said the dentist. Dr. Winter looked in Larry's mouth. "Do you use your toothbrush every day?"

"No," said Larry. "I don't always remember to brush."

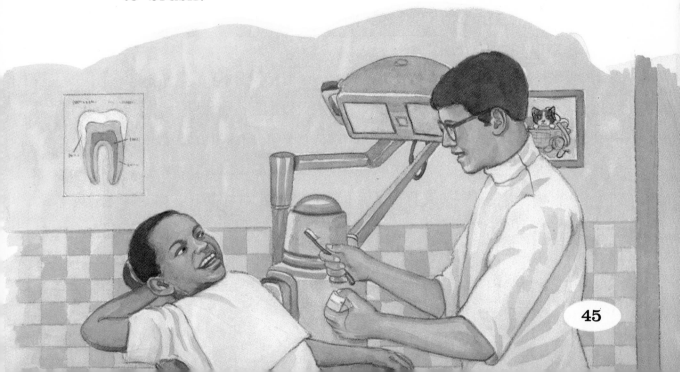

"Do you exercise to take care of your body and legs every day?" asked Dr. Winter.

"Yes, I do," said Larry. "But what has that to do with my mouth?"

"Both are important for your health. If you eat the right food and use your toothbrush every day, you will not get a cavity."

Dr. Winter found the cavity in Larry's tooth. "I will take care of this for you right now. Then your tooth will not ache when you chew your food."

At last the dentist said, "Now your tooth is like new. Now go to that race! Remember to brush every day."

"I will remember to brush," Larry said.

"Come on," said Mrs. Moss. "I will drive you to school."

On they went, but soon there was a noise. "A car can't have a cavity," said Larry's mother. "But this car does have an ache. It drove well before, but now it's stuck."

"If I run, I can get to school in time for the race. Can I go alone?" said Larry.

47

"Yes," said his mother. "Your school is down the street. I will go look for a dentist for our car," she said laughing.

"Cars don't need a dentist," said Larry, laughing, too. "But this car does need some help."

Larry began to run to school. He flew as if he had wings on his feet. He was happy now that he did not have a cavity or a big ache in his mouth.

At school, the children were busy with their work. When Emily saw Larry, she looked up.

"Where were you?" asked the teacher.

Larry said, "I went to the dentist. Then I had to run to school because the car was stuck. I want to be in the race, but I hope I am not too tired now."

"You can relax," said his teacher. "The race will be later."

"I am happy that you will be running in the race after all," said Emily.

"I am happy too," said Larry. "I am very happy that I went to the dentist, too. I may get an ache or two by running, but that will not be like the ache in my tooth."

Questions

Read and think.
1. What did Larry like to do best of all?
2. Why did Larry go to see Dr. Winter?
3. What did Dr. Winter say Larry should do every day?
4. Why didn't Larry want to see Dr. Winter before he went to school?

PREPARING FOR READING

Learning Vocabulary

Listen for short vowels.

fish

air	wish	pitcher	pilot
with	lights	inches	friend

Read the sentences.

1. A visit to the dentist is very important.
2. The dentist will look at your teeth and gums.
3. The dentist will teach you how to keep them clean by brushing every day.

visit   teeth   gums   clean

Developing Background

Read and talk.

Your Mouth

Many people visit the dentist to see about their teeth, but now we know how important it is to look at gums, too. It is as important to clean around the gums as it is the teeth. Decay can come from germs in your mouth. Decay can make a cavity in your tooth, and hurt gums, too. If you use floss and brush around your gums, you will keep germs away.

In *Keeping Your Best Smile*, read about how your teeth and gums are important to your good health.

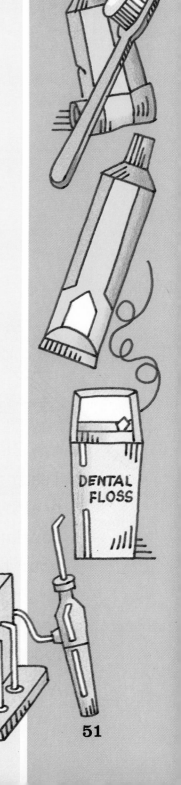

DENTAL FLOSS

Keeping Your Best Smile

Adair Sirota

Clean teeth are important for your smile. Teeth work to keep your body in the best of health, too. It is important to visit the dentist. There you will learn to take care of your teeth.

You need the right food to help your body grow. You need your teeth to chew that food. Then your body can use it to help keep you strong.

Each tooth is different. Some teeth work to chew food. Your teeth do their best work when they all work together.

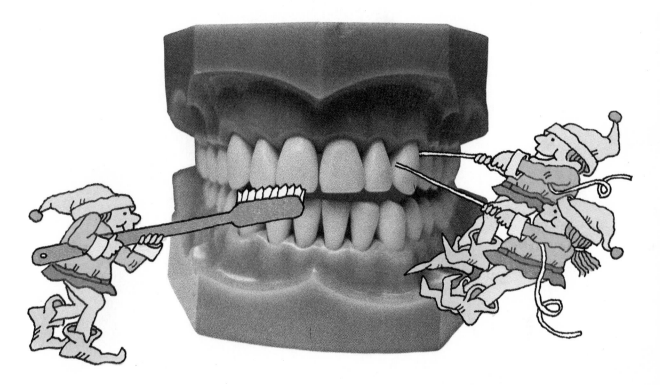

Teeth sit in the gums. The hard enamel on your teeth can keep germs out. Brushing your teeth helps take away food that can hide in teeth and gums. If you don't brush every day, germs will make decay in the enamel of teeth. Enamel is strong, but decay can hurt it. Decay can make a cavity in a tooth, or it can make gums ache.

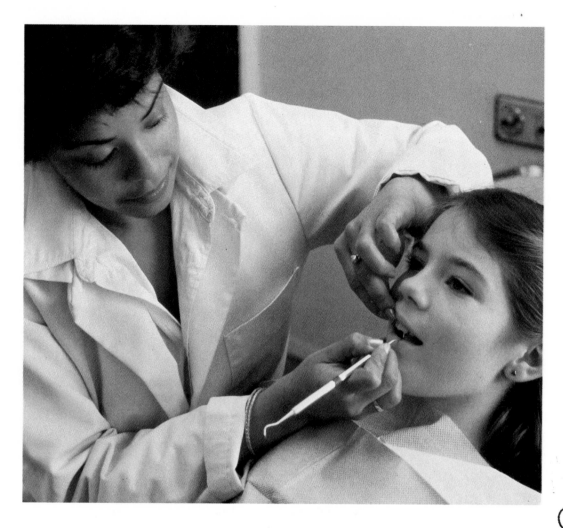

When you visit the dentist, she looks
at your mouth. She can see if your teeth
and gums are clean. She can look for
tooth decay.

The dentist will clean your teeth. She
will show you how to brush with care. She
will show you how to use floss, too.

DENTAL
FLOSS

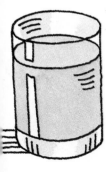

Brushing around all the teeth and gums
is important. You should floss right up to
the gums. If you floss up to the gums, the
spots of leftover food will be pushed out.

Remember, it is important to brush and
floss after eating. If you can't brush or floss,
you should drink water. A drink of water
will float the leftover food away, too. Your
mouth will feel fresh and clean.

Your smile is very special. When you care for your teeth and gums, you care for your smile. When you take care of your teeth, you take care of your body too. Remember these three important things for good health.

1. Stop tooth decay by brushing away food and germs that can make a cavity.

2. For the health of your gums, use floss when you can.

3. Always visit the dentist. She will help you by keeping both your teeth and gums clean.

If you remember to care for your teeth, your teeth will last a long, long time. Your special smile will always be there with a big hello.

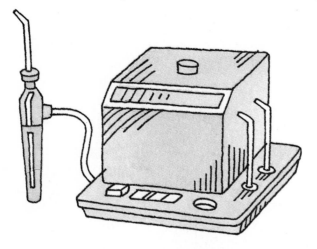

Questions

Read and think.

1. What can germs do to a tooth?
2. What should you do if you can't brush or floss after eating?
3. What three things should you do to help keep your teeth strong?
4. How do your teeth help to keep your body strong?

PREPARING FOR READING

Learning Vocabulary

Listen for short vowels.

t<u>o</u>p

box	cows	doctor	rock
hour	cold	soccer	do

Read the sentences.

1. I will be <u>honest</u> when I say I do not like to go to the dentist.
2. As I <u>recall</u>, I have not <u>been</u> there for a long time.
3. The dentist will <u>give</u> you a toothbrush and clean your teeth.
4. Because I did not go, I had <u>five</u> teeth with decay.

honest   recall   been   give   five

Developing Background

Read and talk.

Dino the Dinosaur

I am Dino. I am a dinosaur in this museum. As you can see, I am a huge fossil. Can you find out how big I am? People come from all over the world to see me. I like my home here, but, to be honest, I don't feel too well right now. When I was out and about, I liked to eat all the animals I could find. Can you find out what kinds of animals a dinosaur may eat? Well, to go on, today I can't chew at all. What is the mystery? Read this play and you will see.

A HUGE TOOTHACHE

Susan Nanus

Players
Bonnie: The Bear
Gina: The Giraffe
Lionel: The Lion
Annie: The Ostrich
Felipe: The Fox
Dino: The Dinosaur
Murray: The Mouse

Setting
A Museum
With Animals

(*It is night.
The animals are
in their places
in the museum.*)

Dino: Oh! Oh!

Lionel: (*Lionel sits up and looks around.*) What is that strange noise?

Dino: Oh! Oh!

Annie: It's very strange. What can it be?

Lionel: Well, it's not roaring.

Felipe: It's not laughing. What can it be?

Dino: Oh! My tooth!

Bonnie: (*To Lionel*) What did you say?

Lionel: Me? I didn't speak.

Annie: Yes, you did. Be honest.

Lionel: No, I didn't. This is scary. Who can be speaking that we can't see?

Gina: Well, who did? This is a mystery. Bonnie? Annie? Lionel? Felipe?

Dino: It's no mystery. Look up here.

(*All five animals turn and look at Dino.*)

Dino: Hello. I am Dino.

Annie: It's the huge dinosaur!

Lionel: But a dinosaur can't speak. This is a trick! Who is speaking for him?

Dino: Oh, no. As one of an honest dinosaur family, let me say, this is not a trick. I may be a fossil, but I can speak as well as the five of you.

Bonnie: You have been in the museum for a long time, and I can't recall you speaking before.

Dino: I didn't have a toothache before. Take a look at my teeth.

Annie: They are huge.

Dino: My toothache is huge, too!

Felipe: You must have a huge cavity in that huge tooth.

Dino: What can you do to help me?

Bonnie: I think you might have to clean out your tooth with a toothbrush, Dino.

Gina: A toothbrush for a dinosaur? It will have to be five feet long.

Annie: What about that brush they use for sweeping the dinosaur collection?

(*They all look at a big brush by the fossil collection.*)

Bonnie: That will work very well. (*Bonnie brings over the brush.*) Here, Dino. Brush your tooth with this.

Dino: I can't. It will hurt too much.

Gina: But your tooth will feel better.

Dino: I know, but I can't do it. Can one of you brush my teeth for me?

Felipe: Come on, Dino. Don't be scared.

Dino: I am a fossil. If you recall, you must give a fossil special care.

Bonnie: Like brushing their teeth?

Dino: Yes.

Gina: Don't be scared, Dino. We will think of something to help you.

Dino: You will? Thank you, thank you.

Lionel: We will if we can. Brushing Dino's teeth might be too hard for us.

Felipe: Too hard? Why?

Lionel: One, Dino's mouth and teeth are up there. Two, we are down here. And three, if we can't get up to him, we can't brush his teeth.

(*They all look up at Dino.*)

Bonnie: Lionel is right. Dino is huge. How will we get up to his tooth?

Gina: Lionel, can you jump up?

Lionel: I can't jump that high.

Annie: What about Bonnie or Felipe? Can you two use your claws to move up his legs?

Felipe: We can try. (*Felipe and Bonnie use their claws to move up Dino's legs.*)

Dino: Stop! Now my legs will hurt, too. (*Felipe and Bonnie stop.*)

Gina: What about you, Annie? An ostrich has wings. Can you fly up to Dino?

Annie: I might have wings, but you know my wings are not for flying.

Bonnie: What about you, Gina? A giraffe is pretty big. Can you get up there?

Gina: No, Bonnie, as big as I am, I can't get up there. It's no use. We can't help.

Dino: Oh, but you have to!

Gina: We want to help you, Dino, but. . .

(*Murray the Mouse comes out.*)

Murray: May I be of help?

(They all look at Murray.)

Lionel: Look! A mouse.

Murray: Not a mouse. A mouse dentist.

All: DENTIST?

Murray: Oh, yes. I am Murray the Mouse Dentist, and I know all about teeth.

Dino: Can you make my tooth feel better?

Murray: I have not worked on a tooth that big before, but I will try.

Felipe: I can't recall speaking to a mouse dentist before.

Murray: That is because I am the first mouse dentist in the world. Now, if you will please give me some help with this rope, I will go to work.

(*Murray brings out a rope.*)

Dino: (*Scared*) A rope? What for?

Murray: I need to get the brush up to your mouth so I can clean out your tooth.

Lionel: How will you do it, Murray?

Murray: Well, I am little so I can run up Dino's tail to his mouth. (*Murray does this.*)

Murray: I have been in funny places, but it is very strange up here.

Dino: Please can you help me now?

Murray: Now friends, the brush please.

(*The animals put the rope around the brush. Murray brings it up.*)

Murray: Now I have it, but I do need something.

Annie: What is that?

Murray: Music.

Dino: Music?

Murray: Oh, yes, music has always been very important to a dentist. How are you all at singing?

(*The animals try singing.*)

Murray: Good! (*He works as the animals keep singing loudly.*)

Murray: There! (*To the animals*) Stop singing, please! (*They stop.*)

Murray: Well, Dino. How do you feel?

Dino: My tooth is better!

Murray: And be honest, did I hurt you?

Dino: No, you didn't hurt me at all.

Gina: Murray, you are the best dentist.

Murray: You have to be the best when you are the first mouse dentist in the world.

Dino: How can I thank you?

Murray: You don't have to thank me.

Annie: What can we give you?

Murray: Well, there is something I want.

Felipe: What?

Murray: Friends.

Bonnie: Friends?

Murray: Yes, many animals do not want to think of a dentist as a friend. All animals need friends and so do I.

Felipe: We will be your friends.

Dino: You *are* my friends.

Murray: Oh, thank you! You have made me very happy.

Bonnie: We now have two new friends.

Annie: A very big friend.

Lionel: And a very little friend.

Dino: And it's all been because of a big toothache!

Questions

Read and think.

1. Why couldn't the museum animals brush Dino's teeth for him?

2. How did Murray get the brush up to Dino?

3. Who are the two new friends that the animals have?

4. Why was Dino scared when Murray said he wanted a rope?

Lee Bennett Hopkins

THIS

I jiggled it
    jaggled it
    jerked it.

I pushed
    and pulled
    and poked it.

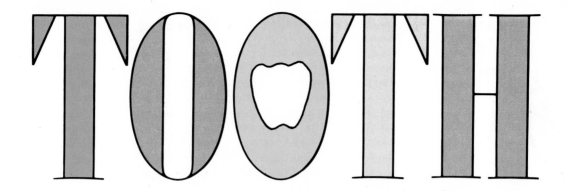

TOOTH

But—

As soon as I stopped, and
left it alone,
This tooth came out on
its very own!

PREPARING FOR READING

Learning Vocabulary

Listen for syllables.

hamster

ham′·ster

relax   ache   claws   animals

fair   letter   giraffe   remember

Read the sentences.

1. The children were very <u>unhappy</u>.
2. They did not do well in the <u>contest</u>.
3. "I can't <u>spell</u> all of the <u>words</u>," one girl said.
4. "I don't want to spell <u>more</u> words now," said the boy.

unhappy   contest   spell   words   more

Developing Background

Read and talk.

A Spelling Bee

A spelling bee is a contest to see who can spell well. At one time in our country, a school might have had a spelling bee every Friday. In each class, the girls might have been on one team, and the boys might have been on their own team. Or there might have been boys and girls on one team. On some days, each boy or girl might spell alone. People came to hear the spelling bee. Today children may be in a spelling bee, too. Luz and Millie are in a spelling bee in the story, *Friends Through a Storm*.

FRIENDS THROUGH A STORM

Argentina Palacios

"Hello. Yes, Luz, she's here. Let me call her," said Mrs. Snow.

"Millie! It's for you!"

"Who is it?" asked Millie.

"It's Luz," said her mother.

"I can't speak to her now, Mother, I am too busy."

"Luz, she's busy now. Please try calling in an hour."

Mrs. Snow had some feelings that something was not right. Weren't Luz and Millie best friends? Why didn't Millie want to speak to her best friend Luz? It was a mystery to her. She had to find out why.

"Millie?. . ." called Mrs. Snow. All was quiet.

"Millie? . . ." she called loudly. No noise at all.

"MILLICENT!!!" she called. "I wish to have a word with you."

Millie looked a little scared when she came down. She was unhappy, too.

"Please sit down here, next to me," said Mrs. Snow. "I want to know why you don't want to speak to Luz. She has been calling you all day."

"Well, I was busy, Mother," said Millie.

"You were? With what?" asked Mrs. Snow.

"I was making a game for one of the computers at school," said Millie.

"You should always have time for your good friends," her mother said.

"The calls weren't important, Mother. She wanted to know how to spell some words in English."

"And you don't want to help her. Is that true, Millie?"

"Well, a spelling bee is a contest," said Millie. "If I help her, she may do better than I will!"

Mrs. Snow said, "I am unhappy to know that you feel like this. A friend is more important than a contest."

"She has asked me how to spell too many words," said Millie.

"It's good that she asked you," said her mother. "*You* will learn how to spell the words better, too, if you help her."

For a time, no one spoke. Then Millie said, "You are right, Mother. Luz is my friend. She is more important than the contest. I don't want to hurt her feelings. Grandpa can help both of us after school. Luz and I will work together."

"You are a good friend, Millie," said Mrs. Snow with a big smile.

Grandpa, who was an English teacher, was happy that the children asked for his help with spelling.

Millie and Luz had to spell the words "feelings," "gymnastics," "laughing," and "through." But they weren't always right.

One time Millie said the spelling of "friends" was "f-r-e-i-n-d-s." And Grandpa said, "No, remember the *i* comes before the *e*."

Then Luz didn't know how to spell "making." Grandpa said, "Remember there is no *e* before the i-n-g."

Grandpa was a very good spelling coach. Millie and Luz had different words to spell each time. Some words were very hard and some words were not as hard. They went to learn the spelling of more and more words after school each day.

The day before the spelling bee, Grandpa said to them, "You two will be the best in the contest."

On the day of the spelling bee, there were five children in the contest. The spelling bee went on for a long time. Then one girl didn't know how to spell the word "dinosaur" and was out.

Next one boy didn't spell "mystery" right. And then a boy didn't know how to spell the word "babysitter."

There were two children left in the contest now. They were Millie and Luz!

"Spell 'babysitter'." That word was now for Luz.

"B-a-b-y-s-i-t-t-e-r," she said.

"Good. The next word is 'hurricane'," said the teacher. That word was for Millie.

"H-u-r-r-i-c-a-i-n-e," said Millie.

"No. Do you know it, Luz?"

Luz gave the right spelling. "H-u-r-r-i-c-a-n-e."

"I am happy for you, Luz," said Millie.

"Thank you, Millie, to you and your grandpa for all your help," said Luz.

"How did you know how to spell 'hurricane'?" asked Millie. "It's a hard word."

"Not for me. I know the spelling in English and Spanish. You see, my home was on the island of Puerto Rico before I came here, and there was a hurricane there."

"What is a hurricane like?" asked Millie.

"It is an unhappy time. A strong wind brings rain, thunder, and lightning. Trees and homes may fall, and people can get hurt," said Luz.

"Were you scared?" Millie asked. She wanted to know.

"Yes, very scared," said Luz.

"I am happy that you didn't get hurt," Millie said.

"Thank you, my friend," Luz said.

"F-r-i-e-n-d," said Millie, laughing.

"Right," said Luz, laughing, too. "The *i* comes before the *e*. Remember?"

Questions

Read and think.

1. Why didn't Millie want to speak to Luz?
2. What did Millie's mother say was more important than a contest?
3. Who helped Millie and Luz to learn their spelling words?
4. Why did Luz know how to spell *hurricane*?

PREPARING FOR READING

Learning Vocabulary

Listen for syllables.

hamster

ham'·ster

contest	teeth	better	cavity
honest	enamel	spread	thirsty

Read the sentences.

1. The <u>winner</u> of the spelling contest should be very <u>proud</u>.
2. <u>Those</u> words in the contest are very hard.
3. The <u>judges</u> say who will be a winner and the <u>reporters</u> write about him or her.
4. As for <u>myself</u>, I like to be in the contest.

winner	proud	those	judges
reporters	myself		

Developing Background

Read and talk.

The National Spelling Bee

The National Spelling Bee in Washington, D. C., is a very important time for some boys and girls. They come from all over the country. Each of those children has been a winner in their home spelling contest. Reporters wrote about them. They worked and worked to spell better and better. They know how to spell many words, but will they know the special one the judges will give them? Now they have come to Washington. In *A Special Kind of Winner*, you will read about one of these children.

A SPECIAL KIND OF WINNER

Cynthia Rothman

Can you remember a time when you wanted to be a winner? You may have wanted to be first in a swimming race. You may have wanted to be the best in a basketball game.

Andrew Flosdorf, of Fonda, New York, wanted to be a winner, too. He wanted to be a winner in the 1983 National Spelling Bee in Washington, D.C.

Before Andrew came to Washington, he had to work very hard. He had to learn the spelling of many new words. He had to use a dictionary to find the spelling of those words.

On the first day of the spelling bee everything was ready. Reporters for the newspaper were there to write and take pictures. Andrew was very proud, but he was scared, too.

It was quiet as the contest began. The judges gave each of the children a turn to spell a word.

When it was Andrew's turn, he gave the right spelling for his word. On his next turn, Andrew was right, too. Then the judges gave Andrew the word *echolalia*.

Andrew looked around. Then he began to spell the word slowly, letter by letter.

"That is right," the judges said.

Andrew was proud.

There was time for lunch before Andrew had to take his next turn.

Andrew began to speak with some of the children around him. They asked him how he did. He began to remember the spelling of his word echolalia.

"Oh, no! One letter was not right," he said.

He went to look up the word in the dictionary. His spelling of the word was not right after all.

What should he do now? He wanted to be a winner. Andrew said, "I have to be by myself and think this over."

Soon, Andrew asked to speak with the judges. Andrew said that he couldn't go on in the spelling bee. He said his spelling of the word echolalia had not been right. Andrew wanted the judges to know what he did. He wanted to do what was right. He didn't want to feel unhappy about the contest when it was all over.

One of the judges, Robert Baker, called those newspaper reporters who had come to the contest. He let them know everything Andrew had said. "I am very proud that Andrew was so honest," he said.

Andrew was asked to be on TV by the reporters. Andrew didn't know why all those people said he was so special.

"One of the things I had to learn for myself was to be honest," he said. "I couldn't feel good about myself if I did something that was not right."

Someday Andrew might be a Spelling Bee winner, but for that day he was a different winner. He was a winner who did his best because he did what was right.

Questions

Read and think.

1. What contest did Andrew Flosdorf want to be a winner in?
2. What did Andrew do when he found out that his spelling of *echolalia* was not right?
3. Why did Andrew want the judges to know that his spelling had not been right?
4. Do you think what Andrew did was right?

PREPARING FOR READING

Learning Vocabulary

Listen for short vowels.

fish

| slide | visit | their | sick |
| think | ice | dinosaur | give |

Read the sentences.

1. Good friends <u>listen</u> to what their friends have to say.
2. They like to <u>talk</u> about the <u>same</u> things.
3. Good friends <u>never</u> talk <u>while</u> their friends are speaking.
4. It is important to do things by <u>yourself</u> as well as with a friend.

| listen | talk | same |
| never | while | yourself |

Developing Background

Read and talk.

May 1, 19__

Dear Sara,

Do you remember when we went to the museum together? Then we went to a lifesaving class to learn swimming together. Next, we played together on the school basketball team. Then, you read the same book that I read. Do you think friends should do everything together? Will we be friends if you take gymnastics, and I act in the school play? Is two better than one all the time? We need to talk about this.

Your friend,

Tina

TWO IS BETTER THAN ONE

Antoinette Bement

Sara went rushing down the street to her friend Tina's house. Sara's mother had said that she could go to the museum after school next Monday, and Sara wanted her best friend Tina to come, too. What a good time it was going to be!

Sara and Tina always did everything together. They were so alike that everybody called them twins. Last summer they went to a lifesaving class together. Now they both could swim and dive.

Sara and Tina wanted to be reporters and travel around the world. They always liked to say, over and over, "Two is better than one."

When they were very little Tina's tooth came out, but Sara's didn't. Sara pushed and pushed at her tooth, but it didn't move. Sara and Tina never wanted to be different at all. They wanted to be the same.

When Sara got to Tina's house, she saw a big truck at the next house. Sara saw a woman who looked busy.

Sara called to Tina.

"Come on in," said Tina.

"Who moved in?" asked Sara.

"That is Mrs. Morris," said Tina. "She's a dance teacher. My mother said I might go to a dance class every Friday. Do you think you can be in the same class with me?" asked Tina.

"I don't know," said Sara. "I never went to a dance class before. I will talk to my mother and father today and see if I can."

"I hope you can," said Tina.

"I do, too," said Sara. "I will talk to you in a little while and let you know."

That night Sara asked her mother and father if she might go to the dance class with Tina. They spoke for a while.

"Yes, you can go, but you must remember this," said Mrs. Kirby. "You and Tina are good friends, and you like to do things together, but you may want to do some things by yourself one day."

"But you know what we always say," said Sara. "Two is better than one."

When Friday came, Tina and Sara were at the dance class. Mrs. Morris was a very good teacher. Tina did every new step very well, and Mrs. Morris said, "Good work, Tina, you are doing very well for the first time."

When Sara did the same new step, Mrs. Morris said, "Keep it up, Sara. Try and listen to the music. You will do better soon."

But try and try as she did, Sara couldn't do each new step.

After a while when the dance class was over, Tina said, "I liked it, didn't you, Sara?"

"Well, it was my first time, Tina. I may like the class better next time."

The next class was not better for her. Tina did very well. Everybody but Sara was doing well. Sara was not happy in the class. She had to do something, but she didn't know what.

What was it her mother and father had said?

They said, "One day you might want to do something by yourself."

Sara had to think about what she should do.

One Friday, Mrs. Morris asked the class to listen to something special. A music club was coming to play for them.

As the music began, Sara began to feel
happy. She liked to listen to the music. She
looked at each instrument. Had she found
something that she wanted to learn to do?

On Monday, as Sara and Tina walked to
school together, Sara said, "I must talk to
you. I have not been happy in our dance
class, Tina."

"I know," said Tina. "Give it some time. You will like it soon."

"No," said Sara. "I have to speak up now. This is the first time we are not both happy doing the same things. We never had to be different before, but this time we have to be.

Dance class is not the right class for me. It is for you. It is time for you to take the dance class yourself, and for me to take the music class."

"Yes, it is," said Tina. "You must do what is right for you."

"And someday," said Sara, "when we have a special show at school, you can dance and I will play the music. So we can always say, 'Two is better than one!'"

Questions

Read and think.
1. What did Tina and Sara always say?
2. What class did Tina and Sara join?
3. What class did Sara say was the right class for her?
4. What had Sara's mother and father said that was a big help to Sara?

CHANGING

I know what *I* feel like;
I'd like to be *you*
And feel what *you* feel like
And do what *you* do.
I'd like to change places
For maybe a week
And look like your look-like
And speak as you speak

104

And think what you're thinking
And go where you go
And feel what you're feeling
And know what you know.
I wish we could do it;
What fun it would be
If I could try you out
And you could try me.

Mary Ann Hoberman

PREPARING FOR READING

Learning Vocabulary

Listen for short vowels.

sun

gums	mouse	quiet	brush
judges	spots	lungs	cute

Read the sentences.

1. What do you think of a boy who gets mud for a king's daughter?
2. He rides a goat up the road, too.
3. The third son in this story is very honest.
4. What will he do with a shoe and a stove?

mud	daughter	goat	road
third	son	shoe	stove

Developing Background

Read and talk.

A Fairy Story

The story, *Hans Clodhopper*, is a fairy story. In this story or one like it, you will find many things that are the same. You may read about a king and a princess. They live in a castle. There may be three brothers. There may be three wishes, a long trip, and a contest. Read and see which of these things you find in this fairy story, *Hans Clodhopper*.

HANS CLODHOPPER

Hans Christian Andersen
Adapted by
Margaret H. Lippert

One day, two brothers spoke to their father. "The king has said that his daughter, the princess, wishes to find the one man who has the best things to say. That man will be the next king. We want to go to see the princess. We want to go speak to her so that she can listen to what each of us has to say."

"I know all the words in the dictionary," said the first brother. "I will say them for her."

"I know what all the important stars in the sky are called," said the next brother. "I will say them for her."

So their father gave a pony to each brother, and they got ready to ride to the king's castle.

Now this man had a third son, too. The third son was called Hans Clodhopper. Hans didn't know all the words in the dictionary. He didn't know all the stars in the sky. Many people said Hans didn't know much at all. When Hans saw his brothers ready to ride away, he asked, "Where are you going?"

"We are going to the castle. The king's daughter is looking for the man who has the best things to say. He will be the next king. One of us will be the winner."

"I want to try, too," said Hans.

"YOU?" they said, laughing loudly. "You don't have important things to say!"

"Stop laughing," said Hans. "You will see. Father, please give me a pony, too."

"No," said his father. "You can't go. You can't be the winner."

"Yes, I can, and I will," said Hans. "If I can't have a pony, I will ride my goat." So he got on his goat and went down the road after his brothers.

"Here I come!" called Hans. He was singing because he was so happy. His two brothers were very quiet. They had to think of good things to say to the princess. Hans was looking all around.

"Hello!" Hans called to his brothers. "Look what I found on the road."

"What is that?" asked the first brother, as he turned around to look.

"A crow!" said Hans.

"What will you do with it?" he asked.

"I will take it to the princess. She may like it."

"Yes, yes, she will like it very much," said the brothers, laughing at Hans. They all went on down the road to the castle.

Soon Hans called out, "Look what I found now!"

"A shoe! Will you take that to the princess, too?" the first brother asked, laughing at Hans.

"Why, yes," Hans said. "She may want it." They went on down the road.

Then Hans called out, "Look at this! One can find so many good things on the road!"

"What is it this time?" asked the next brother, looking at him. "Some brown mud? Will you give that to the king's daughter as well?" he asked, laughing.

"Yes," Hans said, "she may need it. It is good to take everything. You never know what you might need." They went on.

After a long time, they came to the castle.
There were so many people at the castle that
they couldn't get in. Everybody had come to
see the king's daughter. One by one, each
man went in to talk to her. One by one, they
all came out. The princess did not like them,
because not one had important things to say.

At last, it was the turn of the first brother. He went into the castle. He saw the king with his daughter and some reporters. The reporters began to write down everything that everybody said, so it could be put in the newspaper the next day. "What do you have to say?" the princess asked.

The first brother looked around. It was not a cold day, but there was a stove which was very hot. It was so hot that it was hard for the first brother to think. He couldn't remember what he wanted to say. He was scared. He wanted to talk, but no words came out.

"No good," she said. "Take him away."

Then it was the turn of the next brother. He went in. "Well," said the princess, "What do you have to say?"

He was scared, too, but he was not too scared to talk. "It is very hot in here," he said.

"Yes," said the princess. "My father is making chicken to eat."

This brother was ready to let her know what all the stars were called, but he was not ready to talk about how hot it was. He was quiet.

"No good," said the princess. "Take him away, please."

Now it was the turn of the third brother, Hans Clodhopper. He went right into the castle on his goat, singing loudly, "Hello! Hello! Here I come!"

He didn't see the king or the reporters. He was looking at the princess. He was making so much noise and he looked so funny on his goat that the princess was laughing.

"Hello," she said. "What do you have to say?"

"It is very hot in here," Hans said.

"That is because my father is making chicken on that stove."

"Good!" he said. "Then I can make my crow, too!" He went over to the stove.

"But what will you make it in?"

"I can use this shoe I found on the road," he said, and he put the crow into the shoe.

"Now you need something on it."

"I have this special mud," he said, as he put the mud all over the crow. "This will make it good."

The princess was laughing. "You are the man for me," she said. "You have the best things to say, and you can think for yourself! You will be a good king, and we will be happy together."

So that is how the third son, Hans Clodhopper, got the princess and came to be the king, as it said in the newspaper the next day. A strange and funny story you might say!

Questions

Read and think.

1. What did the princess want to find?
2. What three things did Hans take to the princess?
3. Why couldn't the first brother remember what he wanted to say?
4. Why did the princess like Hans?

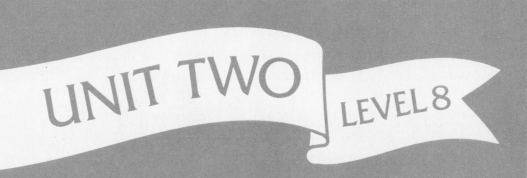

UNIT TWO LEVEL 8

RACING ON

PREPARING FOR READING

Learning Vocabulary

Listen for the schwa.

lion

li'·on

circus	never	about	scream
woman	mud	talk	chicken

Read the sentences.

1. No one likes to come in <u>second</u> in a race.
2. Remember it is as important to <u>finish</u> the race as it may be to <u>win</u> it.
3. When the race is <u>done</u> and you sit <u>back</u> in your car, you will be very proud.

second   finish   win   done   back

Developing Background

Read and talk.

Together

Doing things together with your family is fun. I am Eddie Conrad. In my class at school, I found out that people do many things together as a family. Burton likes to go racing with his sister. Amanda writes songs with her brother. Fred's father does gymnastics with him. My father is going to help me make something special. Read the *Eddie-Teddie Racer* and find out all about it.

123

THE
EDDIE-
TEDDIE
RACER

Johanna Hurwitz

"Come over here," called Mr. Conrad to his son Eddie. "I want you to see something in the newspaper."

"Look," he said. "There is going to be a soap box derby here."

Eddie looked at the newspaper. "I never went to a soap box derby," he said.

"When I was a boy, I was busy making a soap box racer for myself," said Mr. Conrad. "When it was done, I went racing with all my friends."

"Did you win?" asked Eddie.

"I came in second," said Mr. Conrad. "We didn't get everything we played with at a store then. We had to make our own things. I remember that I had a good time with that soap box racer."

"I want to make a soap box racer, too," said Eddie. "But I don't know how. Will you help me?" he asked his father.

"Yes," said Mr. Conrad. "I think I can remember how to make a racer."

Soon everybody at Eddie's school wanted to make a racer for the soap box derby. Eddie was happy that his father was going to help him. He wanted to have the best racer so he could win the derby.

Before Eddie and his father had time to make the racer, Mr. Conrad had to travel to Wisconsin.

"After I finish my work there, I will come back home. Then we will make the racer," said Mr. Conrad.

"When will you be done?" asked Eddie. He was scared that they might not finish the racer in time. "I wish you didn't have to go away now."

"I will be back home on the second of May," said Mr. Conrad.

Mr. Conrad left for Wisconsin. Eddie didn't know how, but he began to try to make the racer on his own. He went to the store to get a soap box.

"Everybody is looking for a soap box," said Mr. Suarez. "You will not find one because there is no soap box like the one I had when I was a boy. You must make your own box."

Eddie was unhappy. He couldn't make a soap box racer because he had no soap box. His father might not get back in time to help. Then he couldn't go racing in the derby. "I can't finish the racer in time. It will never be done if I don't make it before my father comes back."

Then Eddie saw his good friend. She looked sad, too.

"Why are you sad, Teddie?" he asked.

Teddie said, "I went to the store to get a soap box. Mr. Suarez said I was the second one to come looking in the last hour. He said there was no soap box to be found there at all."

"Mr. Suarez said that to me, too," said Eddie. "We will never finish making a racer if we don't each have a soap box."

Teddie didn't say a word.

"My father was going to help me," said Eddie, "but he had to go away."

"We can work together," said Teddie.

"Will we finish in time for the derby?" asked Eddie.

"We can if we make one racer," said Teddie. "We can make one racer that will be the best of all."

"It will be hard work," said Eddie.

"If we work together, we can finish in time," said Teddie.

That very day, they began making the box. First, they had to measure everything with care to make a good, strong box. They worked for a long time, and they worked very hard. While they worked, they had a good time.

"When friends work together, it is not hard work," said Eddie. "When I talk to my father, I will let him know about our work. I will let him know how we had to make our own box because we couldn't get a soap box. I will say, that we have an Eddie-Teddie box racer. It is better than a soap box one. It may win the race."

"I hope we win, too," said Teddie. "But there will be many people in the race. We may not win after all."

"I don't care," said Eddie. "That is not important to me now. I don't think those people had as good a time as we did making this soap box racer together."

"You are right," said Teddie. "But remember, it will not be a soap box racer."

"Yes," said Eddie. "It will be an Eddie-Teddie box racer. It will be the best racer there is."

Questions

Read and think.
1. What did Eddie want to make?
2. Why was Eddie scared that his racer might not be done in time?
3. Who worked with Eddie on his racer?
4. Why couldn't Eddie get a soap box at the store?

PREPARING FOR READING

Learning Vocabulary

Listen for the schwa.

lion

li'·on

castle	swimming	people	listen
winter	fossil	same	always

Read the sentences.

1. A soap box race is open to everybody.
2. Off the racers roll to try for a prize.
3. The weight of the racer is important.
4. Reporters will photograph the winner.

open   off   roll   prize

weight   photograph

Developing Background
Read and talk.

A Soap Box Racer

When you read the *Eddie-Teddie Racer*, you found out that making a soap box racer will take time, but it is fun to do. If you want to make a racer, you can write a letter to the All-American Soap Box Derby. They will tell you all the things you must do. You may work alone or with your mother or father. Look at this racer. What important things can you tell by looking at it?

WEIGHT – 220 POUNDS

COST – $35.00

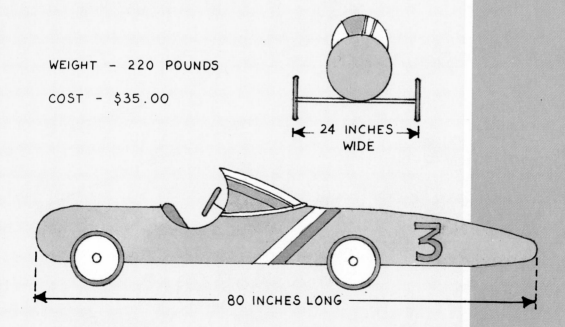

24 INCHES WIDE

80 INCHES LONG

August is a special time in Akron, Ohio. It is the time when many children come to race in the All-American Soap Box Derby.

Children of the United States and the world come to Akron for this contest. To come to Akron, the children have to win a soap box derby where they live. They are proud of their racers. They want the judges to see their work. This is an important race for each of them.

The judges look at each racer before the race. It must have been made at home. A mother or father may have helped work on it. The judges measure each racer to see how big it is. The weight of the car and the weight of the driver can't be under or over a special weight. One race is open to children 9 to 12, and one race is open to children 11 to 15.

Many people come to Akron to see the Soap Box Derby. Some people come because they like racing. Some people come to photograph the race. Reporters come to talk to the children who will be in the race.

When the children made their racers, they had to learn many things. They had to learn the right weight for their racer. Then they had to work at making it roll very fast. They had to learn how and where to sit in the open racer to help it go. This is important because where the driver sits in the racer will make it go slowly or very fast.

Racers in the Soap Box Derby must roll down a special road. The driver sits in the racer. The judges look at all the racers as they get ready to take off. Each driver will try to make his or her racer go as fast as it can. Each driver wishes to win the prize in the All-American Soap Box Derby.

They are off! More than one race is run that day. At last the best driver from each race is ready to try to win first place in the derby. People photograph the racers as they come down in the last race. The best driver is the one who can make the racer roll very fast. The first driver over the finish line will win the race.

When the race is over, the judges say
which racer is the winner. That driver will get
a special prize. Reporters photograph both the
racer and the driver for the newspaper and TV.

The children who did not win can come
back and try to win a prize next summer. For
now, they must go back to work on their
racers. They will try to make them better.
They may try to make them new and different.
At home, they will remember the feelings they
had as their racers were off and rushing to the
finish line.

Questions

Read and think.

1. Why do many people go to Akron, Ohio, in August?
2. What things must the children learn about before they can be in the race?
3. Why is where the driver sits so important?
4. Why do the judges look at each racer before the race?

PREPARING FOR READING

Learning Vocabulary

Listen for prefix: un.

un + happy = <u>un</u>happy

To be <u>un</u>happy is to be <u>not</u> happy.

un + snap = <u>un</u>snap

un + true = <u>un</u>true

Read the sentences.

1. I am very unhappy when I see an <u>unsafe</u> car on the <u>track</u>.
2. <u>I'm</u> a driver of a <u>tiny</u> racing car.
3. <u>Again</u> and again in the tryout, I wanted to move in <u>front</u> of that unsafe car.

unsafe	track	I'm
tiny	again	front

Developing Background

Read and talk.

Racing

The Soap Box Derby race is fun to be in and fun to see. A soap box racer is very small, but, as you can see, you can race in a big car, too. This car may look unsafe, but it is not if you drive well. Before the race began, the driver looked over the car from front to back. Then the driver got in and away he went, in and out, up and down, around the track.

In *A Day at the Race*, Denise Duck and Oliver Ostrich go to the track, too. They see a tiny car in a very fast race. Who will win?

A DAY AT THE RACE

Stephanie Calmenson

One day Denise Duck read about a race in the country newspaper. It said:

BIG RACE TODAY

Come one! Come all! Who will win the big race today? Will it be Roaring Rabbit, Flying Fox, Hurricane Hen, or Muscles Mouse? Come and find out who will win the race today at three. Have all your friends come, too!

So Denise Duck called her good friend, Oliver Ostrich, to see if he wanted to come to the race.

"I have not been to a race in a long time," said Oliver, "and I will be happy to come with you."

In a little while, Denise and Oliver were off to the big race.

As they walked to the race Denise said, "I know this is going to be an important race, and I want you to see it with me. We will have a good time there together."

Denise and Oliver found two places to sit right up at the front.

"I'm happy with this place because we can see everything if we sit here," said Oliver. "I like to see everything at a race. I don't like to miss what is going on."

They looked at all the cars down on the track. There was a blue one with wings on it, a red car with a high body, two cars with stickers on them, and a tiny black car. On the front of the black car were the words *Muscles Mouse.*

"What a tiny car he has," said Oliver. "That is the smallest car here. I hope it's not unsafe."

"It may be the smallest car here," said Denise, "but it is not unsafe. An unsafe car couldn't be on this track today. What car do you like best in the race?"

Oliver didn't say a word.

Denise said, "Oliver, are you listening to me? Oh, it's time for the race."

"I'm listening to you," said Oliver.

"One, two, three . . . Go! They are off!" said the reporters.

"There they go around the track. Look at Muscles Mouse in his tiny car. He is in third place now, coming up fast. All the cars are going very fast."

Right then Oliver said, "I'm going to get something to eat. Can I get you something too, Denise?"

"Oh, no," said Denise. "I don't want to eat now because I want to see the race."

The cars went around the track again and again. In a little while Oliver came back.

"You missed so much," said Denise.
"Muscles Mouse was in front, but then
Roaring Rabbit came up in front of him."

"Look," said Denise. "Flying Fox is in
front now. There they go. Who will be in
front next?" she asked.

Then as Denise turned to talk to Oliver,
she saw that he was not there again.

"Oh, no," said Denise. "Not again. Where
did Oliver go now?"

Denise turned to look at the race again,
and in a little while she saw Oliver come
back down.

"Where did you go this time?" asked
Denise.

"Well, after the food, I wanted something
to drink," said Oliver.

148

"What a race this is!" said Denise. "I'm so happy we came today." But as Denise turned to Oliver, she saw that he was not there again.

"Oh, no," said Denise. "He missed Hurricane Hen and Flying Fox when they were up front together in first place."

Soon Oliver came back.

"Where were you?" asked Denise.

"I saw some friends over there," said Oliver, "and I wanted to say hello."

Denise turned to see the race again. Soon it was going to be over, and the racers were coming up to the finish line.

The people were calling, "Come on, Flying Fox! Come on, Muscles Mouse!"

Then Denise saw Muscles Mouse move into first place with Flying Fox. Muscles and his tiny car went by very fast. Then they were over the finish line.

"What a race!" screamed Denise. But when she turned, she saw that Oliver was not next to her again. She was about to go looking for Oliver when she saw him coming back.

"The race is over now, Oliver. Where were you?"

"I was speaking to a man about the car Muscles Mouse has. I found out all about how that tiny car works."

"You missed it all," said Denise.

"No," said Oliver. "I didn't miss it all. I had something to eat and drink. I saw some of my friends, and I found out all about a racing car. I said I wanted to see everything and I did. I'm very happy I came, but I do want to know something, Denise," said Oliver.

"What is that, Oliver?" said Denise.

"Who did win the race today?"

Questions

Read and think.
1. Who did Denise want to go to the race with her?
2. Who came in first in the race?
3. Why didn't Oliver see who came in first?
4. Did Denise and Oliver like to do the same things at a race? What did each one like to do?

PREPARING FOR READING

Learning Vocabulary

Listen for possessives.

teacher   children

teacher's   children's

teacher's book   children's race

Read the sentences.

1. Grandpa's old car was funny to see.

2. Imagine him going around the field in it.

3. Grandma begged him to shut it off and ride his horse.

Grandpa's   old   imagine   field

begged   shut   horse

Developing Background
Read and talk.

Get a Horse!

In the old days, people could travel by train or boat. They could ride a horse or walk. When the first car was made, it was something to see. People didn't like these new machines at first, because they said they were unsafe. Many people screamed to the driver of a car, "Get a horse!" Time went by and, at last, these machines were very important for travel in the United States. In *Grandpa's Special Ride,* Grandpa gets a car, but he wants to drive it like a horse.

GRANDPA'S SPECIAL RIDE

Earl Robbins

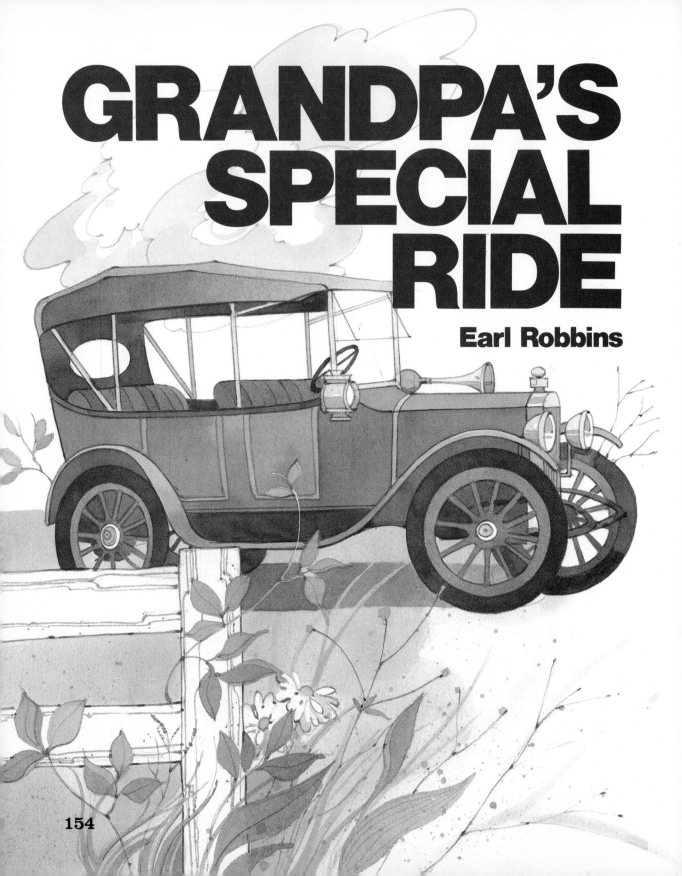

The story my Grandpa tells about the first time he went for a drive in his car, is a story I will always remember.

First I have to tell you about my Grandpa. He was a good driver, when it came to a horse. But, what he found very hard to do was drive a car. It was hard for Grandpa to say, "I can't drive too well." He liked to think that he was a good driver.

Grandpa and my Grandma had a little farm in Indiana. They worked to take care of the farm and the animals all day. When Grandpa needed something at the store, he went on his horse. At that time many people did not own a car. But Grandpa began to think of how much a car might help him with his work. "A horse is strong," said Grandpa, "but it can't do the same work as a car."

Soon Grandpa went looking for a car. He asked his good friend Bunk Selly to help. Bunk had a collection of old cars at the back of his store, and Bunk said he had the right car for Grandpa.

"Come and look it over," Bunk said. "This car will be good for you. It will do everything right, after you learn to drive it."

So Grandpa went to see it. There it was! He couldn't imagine a better-looking car! It was a little old, but it looked very pretty to my Grandpa.

Bunk Selly walked around the car while speaking to Grandpa. He began to show Grandpa how to open and shut things on the car and how to get them to work. He wanted Grandpa to know everything about the car.

"These things are very important to know," said Bunk. Then Bunk said something very strange.

"If you are too hard on the car, it will jump and kick. An old car can kick like a horse if you don't drive it right. You know how a horse can kick."

Then Bunk did something to the car. There was a big roaring noise. The noise scared Grandpa.

"I didn't know so much went into running a car!" said Grandpa. Grandpa got in the car to try it out. He began to imagine that he was the driver, and he began to open and shut things like Bunk did.

"All right," said Grandpa, "I will take it."

Before Grandpa drove away, Bunk begged him to listen one more time. "Please, remember to do all the things I said."

Grandpa drove slowly as he went home, because it was his first time to drive the car. He began to think that after this first ride, he might know everything about the car. That is what it was like after he was on a horse for the first time.

So the very next day, he wanted to take the car for a ride around the field. "An open field will be a good place for me to learn to drive," said Grandpa, "because there will not be a horse, a pony, or people out there."

Grandpa asked Grandma to come to the field in front of their house to see him drive the car.

Grandpa got ready for his ride. Before Grandpa got into the car, Grandma begged him not to go too fast. She didn't want him to get hurt.

Then Grandpa turned on the car, and it began to make a strange noise.

"I can't imagine what that noise is all about," said Grandpa.

"Oh well. Here I go!"

He was off. He moved all the different things in the car. Now the car was making a roaring noise. The car began to move very fast. Grandpa didn't remember that Bunk had said that if you are too hard on the car, it will jump and kick. The car began to jump, and Grandpa had to jump with it. The car was going through the field very fast now.

Grandma screamed, "Stop the car! It's going too fast." She begged Grandpa to stop.

The top of the car was flying up and down. By now, the car was making so much noise that Grandpa couldn't recall what Bunk had said. But right about this time, Grandpa began to think of his first ride on a horse.

"Why is a car so different? Why can't I get this car to run right?" asked Grandpa.

He moved everything on the car that could move.

Then he said, "I will drive this car, or it will drive me."

Off Grandpa and the car went around and around. In and out the field went Grandpa's car, going up and down.

Grandma was screaming all the time, "Stop the car. Please stop the car!"

It was 50 feet to the house when the car gave its last kick. Grandpa and the car came to a stop. A roaring noise was the last noise that came out of the car as Grandpa's ride was over at last.

"Well, I did finish my ride," said Grandpa, as he shut off all the things in the car.

"Yes, you did. Yes, you might say you did," said Grandma.

When Grandpa got out of the car, he turned to Grandma and said, "That was a good ride, but I think I'm happy it's over!"

"I know I am," said Grandma, with her first smile of that hour.

Questions

Read and think.
1. Where did Grandma and Grandpa live?
2. Who did Grandpa go to see to get a car?
3. Why did Grandpa think a field was a good place to learn to drive?
4. Why did Grandma want Grandpa to stop the car?

WRITING ACTIVITY

WRITE A DESCRIPTION

Prewrite

What a ride Grandpa had in the story, "Grandpa's Special Ride." In the first story in this book, Eddie's first ride in the Eddie-Teddie Racer must have been special. A soap box racer ride can be fun, too.

Imagine a special ride you might take. You might have a ride like Grandpa's. You might want to ride in a spaceship. You might ride on a giraffe or an ostrich.

Think about what kind of a ride you might take. Think about these questions, and then try to write sentences for a one or two paragraph story about your ride.

1. What will your ride be in or on?
2. What will it look like?
3. Where will your ride take place?
4. When will it take place?
5. Will you ride alone or with someone?
6. What will you do first on your ride?
7. Then what will you do next?
8. How will your ride finish?

Write

1. Write a story about your ride on your paper.
2. Think of a first sentence for your paragraph. You might use this one.

    My ride (in or on a __) was a big winner!
3. Now write your sentences from page 164.
4. If you write a two-paragraph story, your first paragraph could tell about the ride. The second one could tell what you did on the ride and about its finish.
5. Use your Glossary for help with spelling.

Revise

Read your paragraph. Read the questions on page 164. Did you write sentences for many of these questions? If not, you may want to rewrite your story and put them in now.

1. Did you indent the first word in a paragraph?
2. Did you use correct end punctuation for each sentence?
3. Did you spell words correctly?

PREPARING FOR READING

Learning Vocabulary

Listen for possessives.

Grandpa's   reporters'
Grandpa's car   reporters' pictures

Read the sentences.

1. The women's race looked very unsafe, but it was not.
2. First each rider galloped her horse around the track.
3. Then the women galloped right to the big barrel on the track.

women's   rider   galloped   barrel

Developing Background

Read and talk.

A Rodeo

The rodeo is one big riding contest. You can see a man ride a pony that will try to buck him off. You can see men try to ride animals called Brahma bulls. Brahma bulls are very fast animals. When the ride is over, a man runs out to jump up and down in front of the Brahma bull to keep it away, so the rider can get off and not be hurt. The man may have to jump in a barrel to get away from the Brahma bull. In the story *At the Rodeo*, you will read about a women's contest at the rodeo.

AT THE Rodeo

Debra Desideri

Have you been to a rodeo before? Is this your first time? First time or not, you don't want to miss the women's barrel race. It is a race to remember.

Women come from all over the country to be in this race. Each woman will take a turn at riding her horse around three barrels on the field. Each woman rides as fast as she can. The first barrel is to the right of the racer. The second barrel is to her left. The third barrel is at the front of the field.

To help the horse make a fast turn around each of the barrels, the rider will kick her horse, but the kick will not hurt it. It will let the horse know it is important to keep riding. A rider may bump a barrel while making a turn around it, but she must keep the barrel from falling over. If a barrel does fall, time is lost. A rider may get hurt if the horse runs into a barrel. The women must take care when they ride.

As soon as the rider has galloped around each barrel, she must rush back and pass the finish line. The judge writes down the time for each rider. If two women finish with the same time, they must run the barrel race again.

The women's barrel race is hard work for both the rider and the horse. Before this race, each horse is galloped around a trail to make its legs strong. Then the rider will make the horse do a turn to the left and to the right, as in a race.

The winner of the race will get a prize from the judge. She can be very proud of her riding and of how her horse galloped through the race.

Women in the rodeo travel all around the United States. If you like riding, try to see the women's barrel race. Don't let this fast race pass you by!

Questions

Read and think.

1. How many barrels are there in the women's barrel race?
2. How does the rider make the horse go fast?
3. If two women finish with the same time, what must they then do?
4. Why do the riders try hard to keep the barrels from falling over?

PREPARING FOR READING

Learning Vocabulary

Listen for the schwa.

lion

li'·on

barrel	soccer	unsafe	again
second	open	rider	tiny

Read the sentences.

1. Did you get a letter from <u>across</u> the country?
2. Think how it came across <u>mountains</u> and <u>rivers</u> by truck or plane.
3. In the old days, <u>young</u> boys had to <u>deliver</u> the mail, but not in the same <u>way</u> as now.

across	mountains	rivers	young
deliver	way		

Developing Background

Read and talk.

A Pony Express Map

At one time, the Pony Express was an important way to deliver the mail in the United States. The story, *The Pony Express*, will tell you about it. This map will show you where the Pony Express went. As you can see, it began in Missouri. Look at the stations on the map. What are some of the places the Pony Express went? What city did it go to in California?

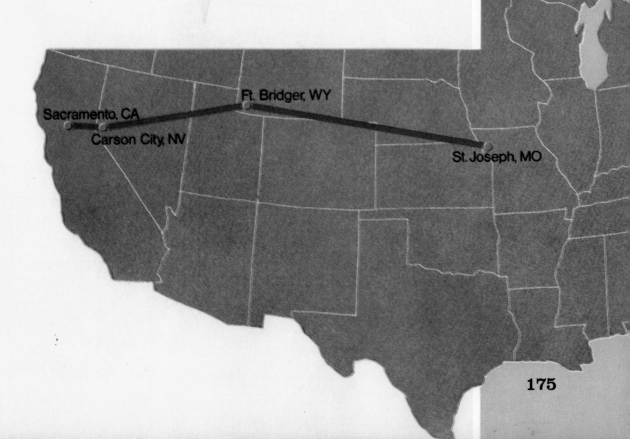

Sacramento, CA

Carson City, NV

Ft. Bridger, WY

St. Joseph, MO

THE PONY EXPRESS

LISBETH STERN

Can you imagine riding a race on a horse all day? At one time in our country, young riders did this. They were racing to help deliver the mail.

In 1860, you could not go from New York to California by train. The train went from New York to Missouri. Then you had to go by stagecoach to California. The mail went this way, too.

These trips were very long. There were rushing rivers to ride across. There were mountains to ride over or around. In the winter, snow and ice made the mountains and rivers hard to get across. People said there had to be a better way to deliver the mail.

Then William Russell said that he had a way to deliver the mail in better time. He could get riders on very fast horses to deliver the mail to California. Young boys who were very good riders made the trips. This is how the Pony Express began.

The mail was put into a special bag called
a mochila. The mochila had two places in it
for the mail. It went across the horse in front
of the rider. It was not too hard to take off the
mochila and put it on a new horse.

There were 190 stations that the riders could use on their trips. At each station, there were people who had to look out for the rider. Because time was so important, each rider had to make a noise before he got to the station. The noise let people know it was time to get a fresh horse ready. As soon as the rider came into a station, he jumped from his horse. He put the mochila on the new horse. Then he was off again! What a race!

PONY
EXPRESS

181

The young boys galloped across the country day and night. Many of the riders went for a long time before they were tired and needed to stop. But the horses couldn't run for as long as the riders. They needed to stop for water. That is why there were so many stations.

The Pony Express riders could deliver the mail in much better time than a stagecoach. But the Pony Express did not run for very long. Soon mail began to move by train across the mountains and rivers to California.

The next time you get a letter in the mail, think of all those fast young riders of the Pony Express.

The Pony Express was very special in the story of our country.

Questions

Read and think.
1. In 1860, how did the mail go from New York to California?
2. Who came up with a better way to deliver mail?
3. Why were there so many Pony Express stations?
4. Why didn't the Pony Express last for very long?

PREPARING FOR READING

Learning Vocabulary

Listen for possessives.

bear   women

bear's   women's

bear's claws   women's race

Read the sentences.

1. My frog's jump is better than your frog's jump.

2. He'd leap over a barrel if I asked him.

3. At the jumping contest this year, he added three feet to his jump.

frog's   he'd   leap   year   added

Developing Background

Read and talk.

Jan's Frog

I am Jan, and I have a strange pet. My pet is a tiny green frog. I call her Jennifer. My grandpa and I found her in the water in the woods. She is about 5 inches long. She has long legs and when she wants to, can she jump! Frogs get their food because they can leap so well. Frogs can hear very well, and that helps Jennifer and me in the story, *Jumping Jennifer*.

JUMPING JENNIFER

NANCY WHISLER

CALAVERAS

Every year, many people come to the city of Angel's Camp, California, to see the Calaveras County Fair. What is so special about this fair?

The Calaveras County Fair has all the things you might think a fair should have. It has a rodeo, a music show, and rides. What is special about this fair is the frog jumping contest. This contest began back in the year 1928. A long time before that, a man called Mark Twain began to write a story about the jumping frog of Calaveras County. Many people know about the contest today because of that story.

Jan had read about the jumping frog contest, every year in the newspaper. This year, Grandpa said he'd take her to see it.

Jan and her Grandpa wanted to learn about the contest. They found out that each frog could take three jumps. The judges measure each of the frog's jumps. They see how many feet the frog went from where it began. There is a prize for the frog with the best leaps.

When Jan found out that children can jump frogs, too, she asked Grandpa if she might do it. Grandpa wanted to get Jan a frog that might be a winner like Calaveras Express, the first prize winner last year. Time was running out, so he'd have to give her a small frog called Jumping Jennifer.

Grandpa said, "We have so much work to do. We have one day to train, exercise, and get her ready. We have to learn how to make Jumping Jennifer leap, too."

People do their own special things to try to make their frogs leap. You can see them screaming, blowing, and speaking to their frogs. One man gave his frog a tap with a ruler. But these things don't always work. People don't know what works best.

As they drove into Angel's Camp, Jan saw a strange collection of frogs. She couldn't remember when she had seen so many in one place before. Young and old people from all over the world were there with their frogs. They were there to try to win the contest.

The contest began the next day. A frog called California King was the first to take three jumps. The judges had to measure the jumps. The frog's leaps added up to 16 feet 8 inches. Next, Green Lightning jumped. That frog's leaps added up to 14 feet.

All the people were very quiet for the next jump. Calaveras Express jumped as if it had wings. Its leaps were the best after three jumps. They added up to 19 feet!

Jumping Jennifer was the last frog to jump. Jan put her foot down loudly, and the first jump was 10 feet 3 inches. She put her foot down again, but the frog's second jump was 7 feet, *back* to Jan. With that jump, Jan lost the hope she had for a prize.

At that second, a huge plane came roaring over Angel's Camp. The noise scared Jumping Jennifer. She flew high into the air for a very, long, third jump of 16 feet. The judge said he'd have to measure.

Then he said, "We have a new winner this year! Jan and her frog Jumping Jennifer win the first prize. Jumping Jennifer's three leaps added up to 19 feet 3 inches."

Right away newspaper reporters wanted pictures. They asked Jan what she wanted to do with the $500.00 prize.

"I want to come back next year to the Calaveras County Fair and try again. I want Jumping Jennifer to make the very best leaps in the world," Jan said laughing. "So I will need this prize to get a plane to fly over Angel's Camp again at the right second to make my frog jump."

Questions

Read and think.
1. How many jumps did each frog get to make?
2. Who had been the winner of the jumping contest last year?
3. Why did Jumping Jennifer jump so well on her third jump?
4. What did Jan say she was going to do with the $500 prize?

THE FROG AND I

The frog and I,
the frog and I
can sing and hop
but cannot fly.

We both can dive,
we both can swim
(although I can't
compete with him).

We both have skin
that's on to stay,
but mine's not *green*,
I'm glad to say.

Aileen Fisher

PREPARING FOR READING

Learning Vocabulary

Listen for prefix: re.

re + mail = remail

To remail is to mail something again.

re + do = redo

re + read = reread

Read the sentences.

1. The little animals wanted to return to their homes.
2. They had been dreaming about it.
3. They must practice jumping over the fence.
4. How excited they were to think about going home.

return   dreaming   practice
fence   excited

Developing Background

Read and talk.

Bambi

Bambi was a beautiful little deer. The book, *Bambi*, by Felix Salten, is the story of this buck. Bambi is the king of the woods. He has many friends there. All the animals like Bambi and in return, he helps care for them. In the book *Bambi's Children*, you can read about Bambi and Faline, and their children Geno and Gurri. This story is adapted from that book.

BAMBI'S
CHILDREN

by Felix Salten
Adapted by Margaret H. Lippert

Bambi and Faline were proud of Geno and Gurri, their children. Faline had worked with them day and night. She wanted the little deer to know how to listen with care. She wanted them to know how to run like the wind. She made them practice all these things and more, over and over.

"One, two, three, GO!" said Gurri, Bambi's daughter. She and her brother, Geno, were racing to the tree. As always, Gurri got there first.

"You are the winner again," screamed Geno. "You run as fast as lightning. I will never get you."

"You will if you try every day," Gurri said. "That is why I can run so fast. I practice all the time."

It was true. The little buck saw his sister practice every day. She was the fast one in the family.

One day Bambi said to his children, "Your mother and I must be away from you for a time."

"Why?" asked Geno.

"It is our way. Your mother showed you
how to be on your own. Now it is time for you
to be in the woods on your own."

The next day, Bambi and Faline left their
children alone. "Be good," Bambi said. "We
will return at night."

Geno and Gurri went to play, brushing
through trees on their way. When they were
tired of running and jumping in the fresh air,
they began to eat. Because both of them were
busy eating by some rocks, they did not see a
fox coming slowly through the trees. They did
not see the fox stop to look at them. The fox
wanted lunch, too.

As he was ready to jump, they turned and saw him, but the fox was too fast. Gurri was right next to him. He got his teeth into her leg, and she screamed. When Geno saw that his sister was hurt, he went to get help.

But Geno and Gurri had not been alone with the fox. A noise like thunder came through the woods. Gurri saw the muscles of the fox relax. She saw the body slide slowly to the ground. He did not move again.

A man came up to Gurri. She was scared and wanted to run away, but she was hurt and couldn't move. The ache in her leg was strong.

The man looked down at her and said, "It was good that I saw the fox was ready to jump. I am happy that I was here in time to help you. The muscles in your leg are hurt, but I will nurse you back to health."

Because Gurri couldn't move, she had to let the man pick her up and take her away.

When Geno and his mother came back and saw the body of the fox upon the ground, they looked and looked for Gurri, but they couldn't find her.

"Your father will know what to do," said Faline. "Go and find him." So the little buck went to look for Bambi.

The man walked slowly to his house with Gurri. He put her down upon his bed to clean her leg with water from a pitcher. When he was done, he gave her food to eat. "There, there," he said. "You need not be scared now." Then he moved her to an open space with a high fence around it.

"Sad little deer, I will keep you here," he said. "I have to go in now, but I will come back every day to feed you. When you are well again, I will let you go."

Gurri looked as the man walked away. She didn't know what he had said. She was all alone for the very first time, and she was scared. She was in a strange place, and she couldn't get out. She wanted her mother and father, and her brother. She wanted to return home. She found it hard to relax, but at last, she went to sleep, dreaming of her family.

Gurri got better slowly. Soon she could get up and walk. Then every day after that, she walked around and around.

One day she said, "I feel better now, and today I will try to run."

She did run a little and then she got tired. She was very excited to think that she could run again.

"I wish Geno were here," she said. "I miss him, and I miss racing with him. I must get out of here so that I can go run in the woods again."

That night, Gurri was tired and went to sleep. While she was sleeping, there was a noise in the trees. She looked up and saw a big buck leap over the fence.

"FATHER!" she screamed loudly, jumping up as she saw Bambi. "Am I dreaming?"

"No, my daughter, you are not dreaming. I am here."

"How did you find me?"

"For many days I have been running through the woods, looking for my lost daughter. At last I have found you. I am so excited because now you can return home with me."

"But Father, I can't return because I can't jump over the fence. It is too high."

"You must try, Gurri. Jump as high as you can. Jump now," he said.

Gurri did try. She galloped and jumped at the fence, but she could not get over it. The fence was too high.

Father saw her unhappy look and said, "Don't be sad, Gurri. You know that when you practice you can run fast. Now you must practice so you can jump high. Soon you will jump over that fence. I know you will not give up. I have to go now, but I know that you will be back with us soon."

"Please don't go, Father," Gurri said. "I need you here to help me."

"I must go now, but you can practice by yourself. You don't need me."

Jumping over the fence, he turned to say, "You are my special daughter. I know you will make me proud of you."

She saw him go, but she was not scared now. Her father was right, and she was excited to think about her return.

"With practice, I can jump the fence," said the proud deer. "Before too long, I will be racing with my brother again. I will do it by myself. Father will be proud of me because I did not give up."

Questions

Read and think.
1. Who were Bambi's children?
2. What did the man do to help Gurri?
3. Who jumped over the fence to see Gurri?
4. Why do you think Bambi wanted Gurri to make the jump?

PREPARING FOR READING

Learning Vocabulary

Listen for the prefix: re.

re + turn = return

To return is to turn again or to turn back.

re + call = recall

re + color = recolor

Read the sentences.

1. Many people feel you can't replace the joy of playing some kind of sports.
2. Many children are in sports events, but some don't get a chance.
3. How can we help these children to improve?

replace   sports   events
chance   improve

Developing Background

Read and talk.

A Chance

What kinds of sports events do you like? Do you like running, swimming, skiing or skating? Can you think about what it might be like to be disabled in some way? You might be disabled, but you like all those sports, too. You like to play and want to improve. Because you are disabled, no one will give you a chance. In the story *Special Sports for Special People*, read about some people who did give disabled people a chance to be athletes who can win.

special
sports
for
special
people

ADA B. LITCHFIELD

At one time, many disabled people were left out of sports events. They didn't play on a basketball team. They didn't go skating, swimming or skiing.

They couldn't. They didn't know how to do these sports. Many people didn't want to take the time to help them. Some people said, "Sports are too hard for disabled people to do."

But the people at the Joseph P. Kennedy Jr., Foundation in Washington, D. C., were different. They said, "Everybody has a right to the good feelings and better health that exercise brings. Everybody has a right to try to replace 'I can't do it' with 'I can do it.' All people need is a chance."

Soon many people in the United States and all over the world began to say the same things. Because of what people said and did, things are different now.   Now, we have the Special Olympics—Special Sports for Special People.

In 1968, over 1,000 children came to
join in two events at the first Special
Olympics. The events were a running and a
swimming race.

In the Olympics, they give a prize to
those who win. In the Special Olympics, they
did, too. Those who came in first, second, or
third got a special prize. In these Special
Olympics, everybody was a winner. Everybody
who was in a race had the chance to feel proud
of how well he or she had done.

There were two days of events. In those two days, many of the disabled children did things they had never had a chance to do before. They had a chance to replace the unhappy feelings they may have had before with new and better feelings. They had a good time. Many children went home to practice their swimming and running. They wanted to improve for the next contest.

Disabled athletes train very hard to improve in the sports they do best. Some have two or three sports they can do. Many of these people now have a better chance to win. Important athletes from the world of sports use their time to help them improve. They help them learn everything they need to know about their sports.

Some disabled athletes win a chance to go to the Special Summer and Winter International Olympics. At these events, people from all over the world get together. There are 16 different sports for children. Some are team sports like basketball.

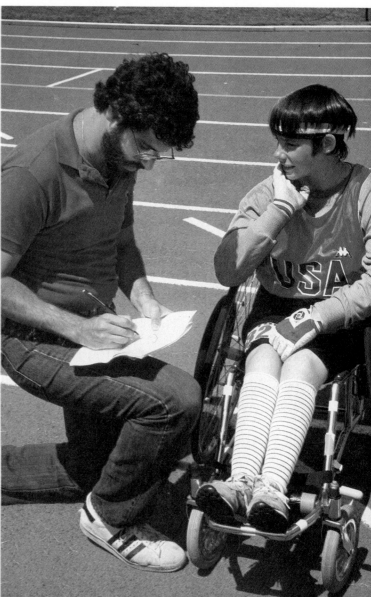

In many places, there are now sports events for disabled people every year. All disabled athletes now have a chance to try. They have a chance to improve in sports.

We know that the Special Olympics brings a joy that we can never replace. It is the joy that comes when you can say, "I am a winner. I can do it!"

Questions

Read and think.
1. What is the Special Olympics?
2. What were the two events at the First Special Olympics?
3. Who gets a prize in the Special Olympics?
4. Why is it important for disabled people to have a chance to be in sports events?

PREPARING FOR READING

Learning Vocabulary

Listen for prefixes.

re + place   un + safe

replace   unsafe

I will replace, or put back, the book.

It is unsafe, or not safe, to ride that way.

Read the sentences.

1. I think it is unwise to be in a race if you are a turtle.
2. I'll never beat many animals I know.
3. Because I am slow and steady, I never need a rest, so I might be a good racer.

unwise   I'll   beat   steady   rest

Developing Background

Read and talk.

The Race

Running a race is work. I'll say that again! Running a race is work, work, work! I am Amanda Giraffe, and I have to make a map of the way the hare and tortoise will go in their race. Look at my map and you can see the track for the race. Can you make a better one? What will you put on it? Now read *The Tortoise and the Hare* and find out who will win the race.

GO

FENCE

WOODS

GREEN TREES

WATER

FROG'S HOUSE

THE FOX WILL BE HERE

MUD IN ROAD

BIG ROCKS

221

The Tortoise and the Hare

Retold by Karen Young

The Hare was very proud of his running, but sometimes he was too proud.

"I can win every race," he said one day. "I can run the fastest, and I can beat everybody." He looked at his strong muscles. "Who will race me today?" he asked his friends loudly.

"I'll race with you," the Tortoise said.

"You? Don't be funny!" the Hare said. "It is unwise to race with me for I am the fastest of all the animals, and you are very slow. I'll be across the finish line an hour before you!"

223

"Let me try," the Tortoise said.

"All right," the Hare said. "We will race through the woods to the big rocks and back. The Fox will be the judge."

Soon they were ready for the race.

"Listen, Tortoise," the Hare said. "Sometimes we say things we should not say. It's unwise for you to race me. If you want to back out, I'll be happy to stop the race."

"No, I will do it," the Tortoise said. "May the best racer win."

The Fox called, "One, two, three, GO!"

The Hare went rushing into the woods. As fast as lightning, he flew to the big rocks. Then the Hare began his run back. As he was running, he saw the Tortoise.

"Hello!" he called out. "See you at the finish line!"

"I may be slow, but I'm steady," the Tortoise said.

The Hare did not listen.

226

"I have so much time," the Hare said. "The Tortoise will never get here so I will stop and rest under these trees." Soon he was sleeping.

The Hare was dreaming about running in the Olympics when the Tortoise came by. The Tortoise saw the Hare sleeping under the green trees. The Tortoise was hot and tired.

"I can't stop to rest," he said. "If I can be steady and keep at it, I can win this race. I'll keep going."

When the Tortoise was inches from the finish line, the Hare looked up.

"Oh, no! Get going, feet!" he said. With a huge leap, the Hare went after the Tortoise, but he could not make it to the finish line in time.

"And the winner is . . . TORTOISE!" the Fox called.

Everybody screamed, "The Tortoise wins! The Tortoise wins!"

"How did the Tortoise beat you?" the Fox asked the Hare.

"It was unwise for me to rest," the Hare said. "Sometimes I am too proud for my own good."

"How did you beat Hare?" the Fox asked the Tortoise.

"I may run slowly," the Tortoise said, "but slow and steady wins the race."

Questions

Read and think.
1. Who wanted to race with the Hare?
2. How fast could the Hare run?
3. What did the Hare do on his way back to the finish line?
4. Why did the Tortoise win the race?

THE HARE

By a ninth-grade student in Swaziland

You are a wonderful creature.
Your mind is full of tricks,
With your eyes so big
With your feet so short and thin.

Who taught you not to shut your eyes when asleep?
Who taught you to sleep at noon not at night?
Who taught you those many tricks you have?
Where do you get the speed you have?

ADVENTURE IN THE NIGHT

BEVERLY CLEARY

Keith and his mother and father had driven for five days on their trip from Ohio. They were tired and anxious for a few days rest when they stopped at an old hotel. What they didn't know was that the room they were about to occupy, room 215, was already occupied. Ralph, the mouse, and his family, had settled in room 215 many years ago, and they were very happy there.

After Keith got used to the idea of a talking mouse, Keith and Ralph became good friends. They had many good times together. When Ralph takes Keith's toy motorcycle for a ride, he has a very exciting time.

Ralph had mastered riding the motorcycle on the threadbare carpet. He went bumping over the roses on the less worn parts under the dresser and the bedside table. That was fun, too.

"Hey," whispered the boy. "Come on out where I can see you."

Pb-pb-b-b-b. Ralph shot out into the moonlight where he stopped, sitting on the motorcycle with one foot resting on the floor. "Say," he said, "how about letting me take her out in the hall? You know, just for a little spin to see how fast she'll go."

"Promise you will bring it back?" asked Keith.

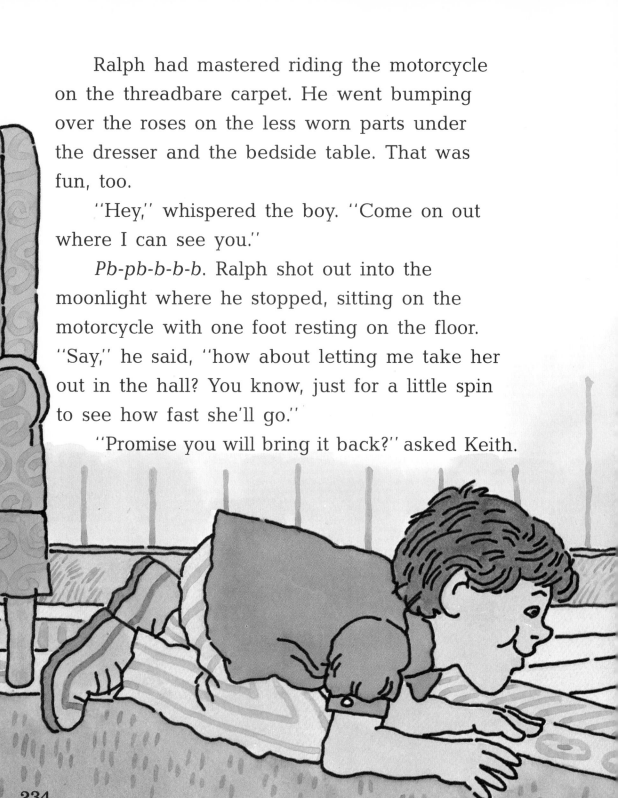

"Scout's honor," answered Ralph, who had picked up many expressions from children who had stayed in 215.

"O.K., I'll tell you what," said Keith. "You can use it at night, and I'll use it in the daytime. I'll leave the door open an inch so you can get in. That way you can ride it up and down the hall at night."

"Can I really?" This was more than Ralph had hoped for.

"You won't let anything happen to my motorcycle, will you?" he asked.

"You know I wouldn't let anything happen to a beauty like this," said Ralph.

"See that you don't. And don't stay out too late." The boy opened the door and permitted Ralph to put the motorcycle out into the dim light of the hall.

Ralph had a scary feeling he was on the edge of adventure. There were no beds or chairs for him to dart under in case of danger. The floor creaked. Someone was snoring in room 214 across the hall. Outside in the pines an owl hooted. It sent prickles up and down Ralph's spine.

It did not take Ralph long to decide what to do. He picked up his tail, took a deep breath. He bent low over the handlebars and flattened his ears. Then he sped down the straightaway as fast as the motorcycle would go. He could feel his whiskers swept back by the force of his speed. It was glorious!

Ralph had never gone so far from home before. The old wooden hotel, cooling in the night air, snapped and creaked, but Ralph was brave. He was riding a motorcycle. He passed room 213 and ran out of breath. He let momentum carry him past another noisy snorer in room 211, and on down the hall to the mysterious elevator that carried people to that wonderful place Ralph had heard so much about - - the ground floor.

When Ralph came to the stairs he stopped to look down, knowing it was impossible to ride a motorcycle downstairs. At the same time he was wishing he could see for himself the wonders that lay below.

Exhilarated by speed, Ralph raced up and down. Once when he heard some people getting out of the elevator, he had to duck behind the curtain of the window at the end of the hall.

Up and down the hall raced Ralph until, after an especially noisy burst of speed outside room 211, he was startled to hear a dog bark inside the room.

Now it was Ralph's turn to be frightened. Oh-oh, he thought, I'd better be careful. If there was one thing Ralph disliked, it was people who traveled with dogs. Dogs always sniffed where they had no business sniffing.

Ralph heard someone moving around inside room 211. Looking back over his shoulder, he saw the door open. A tousled man in a bathrobe and slippers appeared carrying a little terrier. He was walking straight toward Ralph.

Pb-pb-b-b-b. Realizing he was taking a chance, Ralph speeded up the motorcycle. If he turned and headed back to room 215, he would have to pass the man. It was better to continue toward the elevator and hope he could find a place to hide. He raced on down the hall.

239

The wild barks of the little terrier told Ralph that he had been seen by the dog if not by the man.

Ralph reached the elevator where he drove around behind the ashtray on a stand beside the door. He stopped and waited, tense and frightened. Ralph's teeth began to chatter.

The dog whimpered, but the man walked straight past Ralph. He pushed a button, and in a moment stepped into the elevator.

Whew! thought Ralph when the elevator door had closed on the sleepy man and his noisy dog. Maybe he had better lie low for a while. In a few minutes the elevator returned to the second floor. As the man stepped out, the little dog looked and spied Ralph parked behind the ashtray stand.

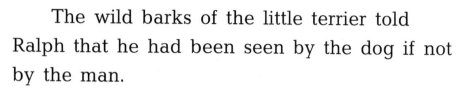

Because the dog was a captive and he was free, Ralph could not resist sticking out his tongue and waggling his paws in his ears, another gesture he had learned from children and one he knew was sure to arouse anger.

"Let me at him," barked the little terrier.

"Cut it out," grumbled the man, fumbling for the doorknob of room 211 while Ralph, a dare-devil now, rode in a giddy circle around the ashtray stand. Who said mice were timid?

The morning song of birds in the pines grew louder than the snores of the guests. Dawn slipped through the window at the end of the hall, Ralph knew it was time to return to room 215. There he was shocked to discover the door shut. Only then did he recall the draft in the night and the slam of a door. He got off the motorcycle and pounded on the door with his fist. What sleeping boy could hear a mouse beating on a door?

Ralph knew from experience that he could flatten himself out and crawl under the door of room 215. But there was no way he could get the motorcycle through the crack, not even by laying it on its side and pushing. The handlebars were too wide.

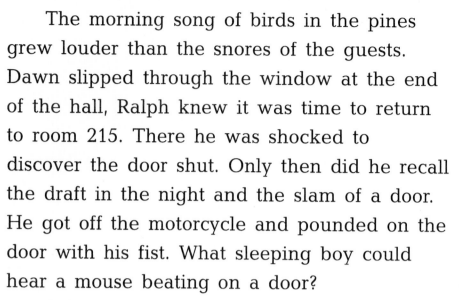

Ralph dismounted from the motorcycle, sat down, and leaned back against the baseboard. He was prepared to guard the motorcycle until Keith awoke and discovered the door blown shut. He was tired after a night of such great excitement and full of dreams. Now that he had seen the hall, he could no longer be satisfied with room 215. It was not enough. He longed to see the rest of the world - - the dining room and the kitchen and the storeroom and the garbage cans out back. Ralph, a growing mouse who needed his rest, dozed off against the baseboard beside the motorcycle. After the experiences of this night, he would never be the same mouse again.

Glossary

A

ache   A pain. After running very hard, Ted had an <u>ache</u> in his foot.

a · cross   From one side to the other; over; on or to the other side. The plane flew <u>across</u> the sky.

added   Put one thing with another; put more onto something written or said. "No," said Mark. Then he <u>added</u>, "Thank you."

a · gain   Once more; another time. Lee kicked the ball once, then he kicked it <u>again</u>.

Ak · ron, O · hi · o   A city in Ohio, in the north-central United States. The All-American Soap Box Derby is in <u>Akron</u>, <u>Ohio</u>.

All-A · mer · i · can Soap Box Der · by   A youth racing program which has been run nationally since 1934. People come from all over the country to see the <u>All-American</u> <u>Soap</u> <u>Box</u> <u>Derby</u>.

al · ways   All the time. Maria is <u>always</u> happy.

An · gel's Camp   A city in California where the Calaveras County Fair is held each year. Jan and her grandfather traveled to <u>Angel's</u> <u>Camp</u>.

ath · letes   People who are good at and trained in sports or exercises. <u>Athletes</u> must work hard and train a long time to be good.

Au · gust   The eighth month of the year. The family will go on a trip in <u>August</u>.

B

back   In the place where something used to be; the part of anything that is opposite the front part. Mark put the book <u>back</u> where he found it.

bar · rel   A large, round wooden container with curved sides. Some people keep food or water in a <u>barrel</u>.

beat   To do better than; defeat. Jim said to Jack, "My team can <u>beat</u> your team."

been   Charlene and Gina have <u>been</u> to the zoo and seen the animals.

begged   Asked; asked for. Tim <u>begged</u> to go to the circus.

best   Paco is the <u>best</u> swimmer on the team.

bet · ter   Sue likes skiing <u>better</u> than skating.

bik · ing   Bicycle riding. Jan and Kim will go <u>biking</u> together.

bod · y   All of a person, animal, or plant. Exercise and good food help Jeff take care of his <u>body</u>.

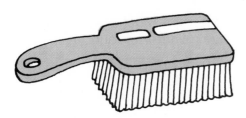

brush   A tool used for scrubbing, smoothing, sweeping, or painting; to scrub, smooth, sweep, or paint with a brush. Paco helps Pilar <u>brush</u> the snow off the sled.

buck   A male deer, antelope, rabbit, or goat. The <u>buck</u> looked with care before going across the open field.

C

Cal · a · ver · as Coun · ty, Cal · i · for · nia   A county in central California. The jumping frog contest took place in <u>Calaveras</u> <u>County</u>, <u>California</u>.

Cal · i · for · nia   A state in the western United States. The Pony Express ran from Missouri to <u>California</u>.

cav · i · ty   A hollow place; hole. The dentist found the tooth with the <u>cavity</u>.

chance   A good or favorable opportunity; possibility. The boys hope for a <u>chance</u> to try out their new boat soon.

chew   To crush and grind something with the teeth. You should <u>chew</u> your food well.

class   A group of students studying or meeting together. The teacher took the <u>class</u> to the park.

clean   Free from dirt; to make clean. Tami helped her mother <u>clean</u> the house.

con · test   A game or race that people try to win. Five children were in the swimming <u>contest</u>.

D

daugh · ter   A female child. A girl or woman is the <u>daughter</u> of her mother and father.

de · cay   A slow rotting of plant and animal matter. Brushing your teeth can help stop tooth <u>decay</u>.

deer   An animal that has hoofs and chews its cud. <u>Deer</u> live in the woods, and they can run very fast.

de · liv · er   To carry or take. People who <u>deliver</u> the mail are sometimes out in bad weather.

den · tist   A doctor who takes care of people's teeth. The <u>dentist</u> told Lisa to brush her teeth every day.

der · by   A race or contest. Paco made a racer for the soap box <u>derby</u>.

dic · tion · ar · y   A book that has words of a language arranged in alphabetical order, together with information about them. You can use a <u>dictionary</u> to find the right spelling of words.

din · o · saur   One of a large group of extinct reptiles that lived millions of years ago. Jenny likes to look at the big <u>dinosaur</u> in the museum.

dis · a · bled   Having a disability. <u>Disabled</u> athletes have special sports events.

done   Finished; completed. Eddie has <u>done</u> his exercises.

dream · ing Seeing, feeling, or thinking about in a dream. While Sara is sleeping, she is dreaming about a princess.

E

ech · o · la · li · a A habit of repeating what is said by other people, as if echoing them. Echolalia is a hard word to spell.

e · nam · el A smooth, hard coating like glass. Decay can eat away tooth enamel.

e · vents Contests in a program of sports; important things that happen. There will be running and jumping events at the track meet.

ex · cit · ed Stirred up; aroused. The children were excited about going to the rodeo.

F

fair Any large showing of products or objects. Rita's class was going to have a book fair.

feel To have or cause the sense of being something; to touch. The players feel good about the team.

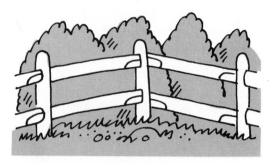

fence A structure used to surround, protect, or mark off an area. There was a fence around the field.

field A piece of open or cleared ground. Anita rode the horse around the field.

fin · ish To bring to an end; come to the end of; complete. Kirk will finish his report by Friday.

five One more than four. The family has five pets.

floss A soft, twisted thread; to use floss. You can use floss to help keep your teeth and gums clean.

Fon · da, New York A town in New York, about 40 miles from Albany. Fonda, New York, was Andrew's home town.

fos · sil The remains or traces of an animal or plant that lived long ago. The dinosaur is a fossil.

fresh Clean, refreshing; newly done, made, or gathered. The children eat the fresh apples.

Fri·day   The sixth day of the week. There will be a ball game after school on <u>Friday</u>.

frog's   Of, by, or belonging to a frog. The <u>frog's</u> home is in the swamp.

front   The part that faces forward or comes first. Linda sat in the <u>front</u> of the bus.

G

gal·loped   Moved or rode at a fast gait. The horse and rider <u>galloped</u> down the race track.

germs   Tiny plants or animals that may cause disease. <u>Germs</u> can live in your mouth and make your teeth decay.

give   To hand over or grant to another or others. Debbie will <u>give</u> Larry a drum for his birthday.

goat   An animal that is related to the sheep. Some people like to drink <u>goat</u> milk.

grand·pa's   Of, by, or belonging to grandpa. <u>Grandpa's</u> house was on a farm.

ground   The part of the earth that is solid; soil; land. The <u>ground</u> was covered with snow.

gums   The pink, tough flesh around the teeth. It is important to keep your teeth and <u>gums</u> clean.

H

hare   An animal that is like a rabbit, but larger. A <u>hare</u> has long back legs and a short tail.

health   The condition of the body or mind. Mrs. Park went to the doctor to see about her <u>health</u>.

heart   The part of the body that pumps blood. Exercise is good for your <u>heart</u>.

he'd   He had; he would. Tim said <u>he'd</u> shut the water off.

hon·est   Truthful, fair, or trustworthy. Jose was <u>honest</u> when he said he had lost the letter.

horse   A large animal with four legs with hooves, and a long, flowing mane and tail. Rita's <u>horse</u> likes to eat apples.

hurt   To feel pain or injury; to cause pain or injury. The dentist asked Ted which tooth <u>hurt</u>.

I

I'll   I will; I shall. "I'll try out for the team if you will," said Jeff to Debbie.

I'm   I am. "I'm the winner!" shouted Pilar.

i · mag · ine   To picture a person or thing in the mind. Can you imagine how it would be to live on the moon?

im · prove   To make or become better. Tina will practice more to improve her skiing.

In · di · an · a   A state in the north-central United States. Bobby's grandpa lived in Indiana.

In · ter · na · tion · al   Having to do with or made up of two or more countries. The class had an international food day at school.

J

Jo · seph P. Ken · ne · dy, Jr. Foun · da · tion   An organization founded in 1946 to help disadvantaged people and their families. The Joseph P. Kennedy, Jr. Foundation created the Special Olympics.

judg · es   Persons who decide on questions and disagreements in a contest or in a court. Mr. Miller and Mrs. Green were judges at the pet show.

L

leap   To jump; a jump. The girl made a high leap as she danced.

lis · ten   To try to hear; pay attention in order to hear. If you listen to what the teacher says, you will know what to do.

loud · ly   With a strong sound. The children in the play must speak loudly.

lungs   The part of the body used for breathing. We take air in and out of the lungs.

M

Mis · sou · ri   A state in the central United States. The Pony Express riders traveled west from Missouri.

mo · chi · la   A special kind of saddle bag. The mochila went across the horse in front of the rider.

Mon · day   The second day of the week. The children go to school on Monday.

more   Greater in number, amount, or degree. Five is more than four.

moun · tains   Land that rises very high above the land around it. The family likes to go hiking and camping in the mountains.

mouth   The opening through which people and animals take in food and through which sounds are made. The dentist looked into Paco's mouth.

mov · ies   A series of pictures on a film that is projected onto a screen; motion picture. Irene likes to watch movies.

mud   Soft, wet sticky earth or dirt. Small children sometimes like to play in the mud.

mus · cles   Parts of the body made up of strong fibers, that help us move and give us strength. Your muscles may ache after you work very hard.

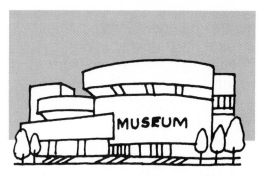

mu · se · um   A building where objects of art, science, or history are kept and displayed for people to see. There are many things to see in a museum.

my · self   I hurt myself playing soccer.

mys · ter · y   Something that is not or cannot be known, explained, or understood. It is a mystery how the dog got into the house.

N

Na · tion · al Spell · ing Bee   A national spelling contest. Andrew went to the National Spelling Bee.

nev · er   At no time; not ever. Joshua has <u>never</u> seen an ostrich.

news · pa · per   Printed sheets of paper that contain news, interesting stories, opinions, and advertisements. Mrs. Jordan read the <u>newspaper</u> every day.

New York   A state in the eastern United States. People could travel from <u>New York</u> to Missouri by train.

nurse   A person who is trained to take care of sick people. The <u>nurse</u> will help Ben get well.

O

off   On the way. The family is <u>off</u> on a trip to Puerto Rico.

old   Not new; having lived or existed for a long period of time. Pam visited a beautiful <u>old</u> castle.

O · lym · pics   A series of athletic contests in which athletes from many countries take part. The summer <u>Olympics</u> were in the United States in 1984.

o · pen   Not shut; free to be used, taken, entered, or attended. The pet contest was <u>open</u> to everybody in the school.

P

pho · to · graph   To take a picture of; a picture made by using a camera. Ted wants to <u>photograph</u> the different animals in the zoo.

po · ny ex · press   A postal service in which mail was carried in relays by riders on horseback. The <u>pony</u> <u>express</u> ran between Missouri and California from 1860 to 1861.

prac · tice   To do some action over and over again to gain skill; the doing of some action over and over again to gain skill. Each boy will <u>practice</u> his singing an hour each day.

prin · cess   The daughter of a king or queen; the wife of a prince. A picture of the <u>princess</u> was in the newspaper.

prize Something that is won in a contest or a game. The first prize in the cat show was a huge box of cat food.

proud Having a strong sense of satisfaction in a person or thing. Carmen was proud of the way she could dance.

pushed Pressed on something in order to move it. Amanda pushed the sled over the snow.

R

re · call To bring back to mind; remember. Anita could not recall where she had left her sweater.

re · lax To make or become less tense. Swimming helps you relax.

re · place To get or give something that takes the place of something else; to take or fill the place of; to put back. Cathy will replace Emily as the dancer in the play.

re · port · ers People whose jobs are to gather and report news for a newspaper, magazine, television, or radio. The reporters wrote down everything the President said.

rest To stop work or activity; something that is left. The team will stop playing for a while to take a rest.

re · turn To come or go back; the act of returning. The birds return to the north every year.

rid · er A person who rides. The rider kicked the horse to make it go fast.

riv · ers Large streams of water that flow naturally. Many rivers run into the ocean.

road A strip of pavement or cleared ground used for going from one place to another. In our country, people drive on the right side of the road.

ro · de · o A show in which people compete with one another in horseback riding, calf roping, steer wrestling, and other similar events. There would be a rodeo at the fair.

roll   To move or be moved on wheels; to move by turning over and over. The racers <u>roll</u> to the finish line!

Rus·sell, Wil·liam   William Russell thought of a new way to deliver the mail across the country. Did you read about the life of <u>William</u> <u>Russell</u>.

S

same   Like another in every way; not another; identical. Jack and Jennifer live in the <u>same</u> building.

sec·ond   Next after the first. Mrs. Andrews read the letter a <u>second</u> time.

shoe   An outer covering for the foot. Andrew had a <u>shoe</u> on one foot, but none on the other.

shut   To close; stop the working or flow of. Mother asked Lionel to <u>shut</u> off the TV.

sick   Having poor health; ill. Rosa did not go to school, because she was <u>sick</u>.

soap box   A box or crate in which soap is packed. Gina looked very hard for a <u>soap</u> <u>box</u> to make a <u>soap</u> <u>box</u> racer.

son   A male child. A man or boy is the <u>son</u> of his mother and father.

spell   To write or say the letters of a word. You <u>spell</u> "gymnastics" g-y-m-n-a-s-t-i-c-s.

spell·ing bee   A contest that is won by the person or team spelling the most words correctly. Bob will learn many new words for the <u>spelling bee</u>.

sports   Games in which people are physically active and often competing with others. Swimming, basketball, soccer, and running are all <u>sports</u>.

stage·coach   A large, closed coach drawn by horses. People and mail went by <u>stagecoach</u> to California.

stead·y   Going at an even rate; firm in movement or position. You must keep a <u>steady</u> beat when you play music.

stove   A large object made of metal, used for cooking or heating. Mother will warm the pot of food on the <u>stove</u>.

T

talk   To express ideas by using speech; speak. After Anne and Tim read the book, they <u>talk</u> about it.

teeth   More than one tooth. A lion has big, long <u>teeth</u>.

think   To use the mind to form ideas or to make decisions. The twins <u>think</u> they are ready to try out for the team.

third   Next after the second. Sam hit the ball on his <u>third</u> try.

those   The coach asked <u>those</u> children who wanted to try out for the team to meet in the park.

ti · ny   Very small. A mouse is a <u>tiny</u> animal.

tired   Worn-out; weary. Tim was <u>tired</u> after the hard exercises.

tooth   One of the hard, white bonelike parts in the mouth. Maria lost a <u>tooth</u>, but she will grow a new one.

tor · toise   A turtle that lives on land. The <u>tortoise</u> moved very slowly.

track   A path, race course, or other trail. The cars race around the <u>track</u>.

Twain, Mark   An American writer. <u>Mark</u> <u>Twain</u> wrote a story called "The Celebrated Jumping Frog of Calaveras County."

U

un · hap · py   Without happiness or joy; sad. The dog was <u>unhappy</u> when the children left for school.

un · safe   Not safe; harmful or dangerous. It is <u>unsafe</u> to go swimming alone.

un · wise   Not having or showing good judgment and intelligence. It is <u>unwise</u> to play in the street.

V

vis·it   To go or come to see. Lisa's city friends will <u>visit</u> her in the country.

W

way   A method for doing or getting something; moving along a particular route or in a particular direction. Walking is a good <u>way</u> to get exercise.

weight   The amount of heaviness of a person or thing. The <u>weight</u> of the box was too much for Ann to move.

well   In good health, healthy; in a good or satisfactory way. Ben and his family are <u>well</u> and happy.

while   During or in the time that. <u>While</u> Kim was skating, Miyo was making a snowman.

win   To do better than any other person in a race or contest. It is more important to do your best than to <u>win</u>.

win·ner   A person or thing that wins. Tina was the <u>winner</u> of the race.

wom·en's   Of, by or belonging to women. The <u>women's</u> book club will meet on Friday.

words   Sounds or groups of sounds having meaning and forming part of a language, or the written letters or groups of letters standing for the sounds. Lars will learn to read the new <u>words</u> in his book.

Y

year   A period of time made up of twelve months. Elena lived in Ohio for a <u>year</u>.

young   Having lived or existed for a short time. A <u>young</u> duck is called a duckling.

your·self   You can do many things by <u>yourself</u>.